Wisconsin

SUPPLEMENT FOR

D1517640

Modern Real Estate Practice

LAWRENCE SAGER

SIXTH EDITION REVISED

Real Estate
Education Company
a division of Dearborn Financial Publishing, Inc.

While a great deal of care has been taken to provide accurate and current information, the ideas, suggestions, general principles and conclusions presented in this text are subject to local, state and federal laws and regulations, court cases and any revisions of same. The reader thus is urged to consult legal counsel regarding any points of law—this publication should not be used as a substitute for competent legal advice.

©1982, 1984, 1986, 1989, 1993, 1995 by Dearborn Financial Publishing, Inc.®

Published by Real Estate Education Company,
a division of Dearborn Financial Publishing, Inc.®

Printed in the United States of America.

95 96 97 10 9 8 7 6 5 4 3 2 1

Library of Congress Cataloging-in-Publication Data

Sager, Lawrence.
    Wisconsin supplement for Modern real estate practice / Lawrence
Sager.
        p. cm.
    "With the endorsement of the Wisconsin Realtors Association."
    Includes index.
    ISBN 0-7931-1324-5
        1. Real estate business—Law and legislation—Wisconsin.
    2. Vendors and purchasers—Wisconsin. 3. Real property—Wisconsin.
    4. Real estate business—Wisconsin. I. Galaty, Fillmore W. Modern
    real estate practice. II. Title.
    KF2042.R4G34   1990 Suppl. 4
    346.77504′37—dc20   93-19039
    [347.7506437]   CIP

Contents

	Preface	v
4	Real Estate Brokerage	1
5	Listing Agreements	8
6	Interests in Real Estate	17
7	How Ownership Is Held	20
8	Legal Descriptions	24
9	Real Estate Taxes and Other Liens	28
10	Real Estate Contracts	33
11	Transfer of Title	46
12	Title Records	52
13	Real Estate License Laws	56
14/15	Real Estate Financing	69
16	Leases	78
19/20	Control of Land Use and Property Development and Subdivision	83
23	Closing the Real Estate Transaction	88
Special Lesson:	Real Estate License Examination	97
	Answer Key	103
	Index	106

Preface

Although real estate activity in the state of Wisconsin is subject to federal laws and regulations, it is controlled primarily by Wisconsin's laws, rules and regulations and by state customs that prevail where no law covers a practice.

This book is a supplement to the text *Modern Real Estate Practice* by Galaty, Allaway and Kyle, published by the Real Estate Education Company. The *Wisconsin Supplement*, which covers the laws, practices and procedures that apply specifically to real estate activity in Wisconsin, is keyed closely to the presentation of the material in the primary text. The information is confined to that not covered in *Modern Real Estate Practice*. Some chapters in *Modern Real Estate Practice* are not covered in the *Wisconsin Supplement* because Wisconsin laws do not vary from their coverage in the text.

Each chapter in this supplement is followed by a test. These tests serve as both learning and teaching devices. As you finish each chapter, and before going on to the next, be sure that you can answer each question and that you understand all the material covered. An answer key section for the test questions is included at the end of the supplement.

The *Wisconsin Supplement* was written by Lawrence Sager. Sager is a licensed real estate broker, certified residential appraiser and REALTOR®, holds a master's degree in urban land economics from the University of Illinois and is Real Estate Coordinator at the Madison Area Technical College. His writings have appeared in numerous publications in the real estate field and related fields.

Sager has acted as a research consultant for the Madison Area Technical College, the University of Wisconsin and other public and private organizations. He is a Certified Fair-Housing trainer and has served as president of the Community Reinvestment Alliance, Madison, Wisconsin. He has worked with the Wisconsin Real Estate Examining Board as a course writer and as the assistant executive secretary in the certification of educational programs for real estate licensure. He is a member of the Professional Standards Committee of the Greater Madison Board of REALTORS®, as well as the Appraiser Application Advisory Committee of the Wisconsin Department of Regulation and Licensing and the Advisory Committee on Continuing Assessor Education of the Wisconsin Department of Revenue. He is the author of the *Guide to Passing the Real Estate Exam (ACT)*, the *Guide to Passing the PSI Real Estate Exam* (1994) and the 1980 and 1983 editions of the *Wisconsin Real Estate Manual*.

We wish to thank John M. Shipley, CRS, Waukesha County Technical College; Hugh Burdick, Gateway Technical College and BOAI School of Real Estate; John F. Wilcox, Chippewa Valley Technical College; Ted A. Perszyk, Milwaukee Area Technical College; and Charles Trester, Northeast Wisconsin Technical College, for their assistance with the sixth edition.

Forms in the supplement are printed with the permission of the Wisconsin Department of Regulation and Licensing, the State Bar of Wisconsin, the Wisconsin REALTORS® Association, the Wisconsin Legal Blank Company and Nelco, Inc.

4

Real Estate Brokerage

In Wisconsin, *a person must be a licensed real estate broker in order to perform, negotiate or attempt to perform or negotiate "FOR OTHERS FOR A FEE" any of the following activities* involving real property or a business opportunity: listing, selling, buying, exchanging, leasing, renting or dealing in options. In other words, a person must have a broker's license in order to operate a brokerage and collect commissions.

Real Estate License Law

Wisconsin real estate licenses are granted and regulated by the *Wisconsin Department of Regulation and Licensing* under the provisions of Chapter 452 of the Wisconsin Statutes. This law and the department's rules and regulations also regulate and restrict the activities of real estate brokers and salespeople. Many of the provisions of this law are discussed in Chapter 13 of this supplement.

Creating an Agency

In Wisconsin, an agency between a broker and seller generally is created by a *listing contract*. The listing contract establishes the relationship between the broker and the seller and defines the broker's right to a commission. According to Wisconsin law, the listing contract must be *in writing, describe the real estate involved, state the price and terms of the sale, state the commission, establish the expiration date, name the broker involved and be signed by the person paying the commission.* If a real estate broker and his or her associates wish to act as agents of the buyer in a real estate transaction, they must use Form WB-36, Exclusive Buyer Agency Contract, or permit the buyer's attorney to draft the contract.

Dual agency. The Wisconsin Supreme Court has ruled that a broker "cannot sacrifice the interests of either party in order to further his own individual interests by attempting to procure double commissions. . . ." Therefore, *dual agency is prohibited in Wisconsin unless*: (1) *the agent acts as a middleman,* introduces the parties and leaves further negotiations to them or (2) *the broker acts as agent for both parties after he or she has made full disclosure* to each of the parties. Dual agency consent must be in writing. The new broker agency law refers to multiple representation rather than dual agency. Section 452.137 of the Wisconsin Statutes states that no broker may provide brokerage services to more than one client in a transaction without an agency agreement with each client and a written consent to multiple representation.

The Broker's Commission

In order for a broker to collect his or her commission, the amount or rate of the commission must be clearly stated in the listing as a percentage of selling price or dollar amount or as a percentage of the

---

This material supplements Chapter 4 in *Modern Real Estate Practice* by Galaty, Allaway and Kyle.

list price if the property is exchanged. The listing contract also must meet the requirements of a valid listing as detailed in Chapter 5.

In any Wisconsin real estate transaction, *the amount of a broker's commission is determined by mutual agreement between the broker and the seller.* The commission usually is based on a percentage of the final sales price. However, the parties may agree on a fixed dollar amount of commission as opposed to a percentage. Either of these provisions, if clearly stated, satisfies the legal requirements for a listing contract in Wisconsin.

Generally, brokers earn a commission by accomplishing what they were employed to do. Under most listing agreements, *the broker must procure a buyer who is ready* and *willing* to enter into a binding offer-to-purchase contract and financially *able* to carry out the terms of that contract and complete the sale.

Broker-Salesperson Relationship

The nature of a real estate salesperson's relationship with a broker is determined by mutual agreement. The actual form of the employment contract between a broker and salesperson will depend on whether the salesperson is to operate as the *broker's employee* or as an *independent contractor.* The distinction between the two is discussed in the text.

Most real estate salespeople in Wisconsin are affiliated with their brokers as independent contractors. A sample contract creating a broker-independent contractor relationship has been developed by the Wisconsin REALTORS® Association. It contains these provisions:

1. The independent contractor must *work exclusively for the real estate company.*

2. The independent contractor must *abide by* the applicable *state laws* and the *rules and regulations* of the Wisconsin Real Estate Board and the Wisconsin Department of Regulation and Licensing, as well as the *Code of Ethics* of the National Association of REALTORS® and its local affiliates. Some contracts specify that the contractor must abide by the company policy manual. This provision, which is optional, tends to limit contractors' control over the details of their work and may call into question their status as independent contractors. Caution should be exercised by both sides in establishing this provision.

3. The independent contractor will be *compensated on a commission basis according to a schedule attached to the contract.* The division of commission set out in the schedule may be altered in special cases by mutual agreement. Commissions are held by the real estate company in the independent contractor's name and paid in accordance with the commission schedule. The company broker may not hold the commissions in the trust account used for clients' deposits.

4. *Expenses charged against commissions will be paid before a commission is divided.* Expenses, therefore, will be shared between the contractor and the company.

5. The independent contractor is *not a servant, an employee* or *a partner* and is solely responsible for reporting and paying taxes on commission received.

6. The *contract may be terminated at any time* by either party upon notice. Termination does not affect accrued commissions due the independent contractor.

7. The *contract* and the *commission schedule* must be *signed* by both parties and *dated.*

Independent contractors should have an attorney review the contract before they sign it so that it can be properly modified according to their particular situations. The broker-independent contractor relationship does not release brokers from responsibility for the actions from their salespeople.

ETHICAL RESPONSIBILITIES OF THE BROKER

Broker's Responsibility for Own Statements (Chapter RL24 of Wisconsin Statutes)

As discussed in the text, brokers make many statements and representations regarding the condition of a property being offered for sale or rent. Because brokers may be held liable for such statements, they must be very careful not to make statements that misrepresent or are not true. To help brokers avoid problems in this area, several rules of practice have been suggested for use by licensees:

1. Brokers should *make full disclosure* of all facts known to them without violating the basic duty of the agent-principal relationship.

2. Brokers should *obtain as much information as possible* from the seller. The law has been requiring more disclosure and requires the seller to acquire facts for the purpose of disclosure, as evidenced by the Seller Disclosure Law.

3. Brokers should *not knowingly make false representations*, nor should they state an opinion without disclosing all the facts that may affect that statement.

4. When dealing with inexperienced buyers, brokers must *exercise extra care in making full and complete disclosures* and must refrain from making statements that generally might be considered as "puffing" or sales psychology.

THE NEW REAL ESTATE BROKER AGENCY LAW

The new real estate broker agency law became effective October 1, 1994. The new agency law identifies specific duties that licensees have to all parties in a transaction as well as the duties to clients only. Specific changes in the new agency law include:

1. Licensees must now disclose as an adverse fact information that indicates that a party to a transaction is not able or does not intend to meet his or her obligations under a contract or agreement made concerning the transaction such as either the buyer or seller has no intention of completing the contract.

2. Licensees must keep confidential any information given to them in confidence or any information they obtain that they know a reasonable party would want to keep confidential unless the information is an adverse fact that must be disclosed or the party specifically authorizes the licensee to disclose it. Licensees must continue to keep the information confidential after the transaction is complete and after their firm is no longer providing brokerage services to the party. This issue of confidentiality is probably the most significant change in the whole law.

3. Licensees may not provide brokerage services unless they or a co-broker have an agency agreement.

4. Before providing services to a party to a transaction, licensees must provide to that party a written agency disclosure form containing: (a) a statement of which party is the licensee's client or if the licensee is providing brokerage services to more than one client, a statement of which parties are the licensee's clients; (b) a statement of the licensee's duties to his client; (c) a state-

ment of the licensee's duties to all parties; (d) any additional information that the licensee feels is necessary to clarify her relationship to her client or customer; and (e) the following exact confidentiality statement:

NOTICE TO CLIENTS AND CUSTOMERS

A BROKER IS REQUIRED TO MAINTAIN THE CONFIDENTIALITY OF ALL INFORMA-TION OBTAINED BY THE BROKER IN CONFIDENCE AND OF ALL INFORMATION OBTAINED BY THE BROKER THAT HE OR SHE KNOWS A REASONABLE PARTY WOULD WANT TO BE KEPT CONFIDENTIAL, UNLESS THE INFORMATION IS REQUIRED TO BE DISCLOSED BY LAW. THE FOLLOWING INFORMATION IS REQUIRED TO BE DISCLOSED BY LAW.

1.   MATERIAL ADVERSE FACTS, AS DEFINED IN SECTION 452.01(5G) OF THE WISCONSIN STATUTES.

2.   ANY FACTS KNOW BY THE BROKER THAT CONTRADICT ANY INFORMA-TION INCLUDED IN A WRITTEN INSPECTION REPORT ON THE PROPERTY OR REAL ESTATE THAT IS THE SUBJECT OF THE TRANSACTION.

TO ENSURE THAT THE BROKER IS AWARE OF SPECIFIC INFORMATION YOU CON-SIDER CONFIDENTIAL, YOU MAY LIST THAT INFORMATION IN THE SPACE BE-LOW MARKED "CONFIDENTIAL INFORMATION" AT A LATER TIME, YOU MAY ALSO PROVIDE THE BROKER WITH OTHER WRITTEN NOTIFICATION OF WHAT INFORMATION YOU CONSIDER TO BE CONFIDENTIAL.

CONFIDENTIAL INFORMATION:

_____

_____

_____

5.   Licensees must enter into an agency agreement with each client and obtain written consent to multiple representation when acting as a dual agent. This written consent must contain state-ments concerning the licensee's duties to each client or party and a statement that the clients understand the licensee's duties and consent to the licensees providing brokerage services, un-less the client knows or should have known of the misrepresentation or the broker is repeating a misrepresentation made to him or her by the client.

Licensees must be especially aware of Chapter RL24, which covers conduct and ethical practices for real estate licenses in Wisconsin. Chapter RL24 requires the following:

1.   Misrepresentation: A client is not liable for a misrepresentation made by a broker when provid-ing brokerage services, unless the client knows or should have known of the misrepresentation or the broker is repeating a misrepresentation made to him or her by the client.

2.   Licensees acting as an agent in a real estate transaction involving real estate improved with a structure must make a reasonably competent and diligent inspection of accessible areas of the structure and immediate surrounding areas of the property to detect material adverse facts. A reasonably competent and diligent inspection of real estate improved with a structure does not require the operation of mechanical equipment; the opening of panels, doors or covers for ac-cess to mechanical systems; or the moving of furniture, boxes or other property; nor does it

require a licensee to observe areas of the property for which entry presents an unreasonable risk of injury or areas accessible only by ladder, by crawling, or other equivalent means of access.

3. A licensee acting as an agent in a real estate transaction must disclose to each party, in writing and in a timely fashion, all material adverse facts that the broker knows and that the party does not know or cannot discover through a reasonably vigilant observation, unless the disclosure of the material adverse fact is prohibited by law. The provision is not limited to the condition of the property but includes other material adverse facts in the transaction.

4. A licensee acting as an agent in a real estate transaction who becomes aware of information suggesting the possibility of an adverse fact material to the transaction will be practicing competently if the licensee discloses to the parties the information suggesting the possibility of adverse facts material to the transaction in writing and in a timely fashion, recommends the parties obtain expert assistance to inspect or investigate for possible adverse facts material to the transaction, and, if directed by the parties, drafts appropriate inspection or investigation contingencies. A licensee is not required to retain third-party inspectors or investigators to perform investigations of information suggesting the possibility of an adverse fact material to the transaction.

Section 452.23 of the Wisconsin Statutes makes clear certain facets of what can and what cannot be disclosed by real estate licensees. Brokers and salespeople may not disclose any information that may result in unlawful discrimination under S.101.22 or unlawful discrimination based on handicap under federal law. For example, licensees may not disclose that current or former occupants of a property suffered from acquired immune deficiency syndrome (AIDS—S.452.23[1]). Section 452.23 also states that brokers and salespeople are not required to disclose the following: (1) that the property was the site where an act such as a murder occurred if such occurrence has no effect on the physical condition of the property (S.452.23[2][a]); (2) information on the physical condition of the property if a written report that discloses the information was prepared by a qualified third party and provided to the appropriate persons (S.452.23[2][b]); and (3) whether the property is located near any adult family home, community-based residential facility or nursing home (S.452.23[2][c]). In addition, a broker or salesperson must disclose any information that contradicts the written report of a qualified third party.

Finally, Section 452.23(4) states that "in performing an investigation or inspection and in making a disclosure in connection with a real estate transaction, a broker or salesperson shall exercise the degree of care expected to be exercised by a reasonably prudent person who has the knowledge, skills and training required for licensure as a salesperson or broker under this chapter." In other words, if a broker or salesperson is not required to have specific knowledge, skills or training to be licensed, he or she will not need that knowledge, skill or training to perform a competent inspection, investigation or disclosure.

Seller Disclosure Law

Chapter 709 of the Wisconsin Statutes requires sellers of one-family to four-family residential properties to provide buyers with a copy of the real estate condition report presented in the statutes. The law covers broker-assisted transactions as well as property sold by owners.

The law requires a seller to complete the condition report with information based on his or her own personal knowledge as well as on information obtained from experts, professionals and qualified third-party inspectors as defined in Section 452.23(2)(B) of the Wisconsin Statutes. The real estate condition report requires the seller to respond to a list of 28 statements concerning the condition of the property. It is the seller's obligation to respond to each statement with regard to the property as "correct," "incorrect" or "not applicable." If a defect is disclosed in the report, an explanation of the defect should be included within the report.

Upon completion of the report by the seller, the seller must sign and date the report, stating that to the best of the seller's knowledge, the information presented in the report is true and correct. Third-party inspection reports relied on by the seller to complete the condition report should be attached to the seller's real estate condition report.

Each potential buyer may receive a copy of the real estate condition report upon viewing a property for sale prior to submitting an offer to purchase. However, a copy of the report must be provided to a buyer no later than ten days after acceptance of an offer to purchase. Receipt of the report should be verified in writing. If defects are disclosed in the report and the buyer did not receive the report prior to the acceptance of the offer to purchase, the buyer has two business days (48 hours) to rescind the offer to purchase. However, if the buyer received a copy of the real estate condition report prior to accepting the offer to purchase, the buyer has no right of rescission via the condition report. Fiduciaries appointed by the court, personal representatives, trustees, conservators, property exempt from real estate transfer fees and real property that has never been inhabited are all exempt from the requirements of Chapter 709.

Broker's Liability for Salespeople and Other Broker Statements

Brokers bear full responsibility not only for any false statements that they may make during a transaction, but also for false statements made by their sales employees and associates, whether or not the brokers had prior knowledge of their misstatements. Under the new broker agency law, the listing broker is not liable for a misrepresentation made by the other broker, unless the broker knew or should have known of the other broker's misrepresentation or the other broker is repeating a misrepresentation made to him or her by the broker.

Mobile Home Sales

In Wisconsin, mobile homes are considered *personal property.* Mobile-home salespeople, therefore, need not be licensed as real estate salespeople or brokers, although they must be licensed by the Motor Vehicle Department of the Wisconsin Department of Transportation. This department also regulates the sale of mobile homes. A mobile home is considered real property when it is affixed to the land and is sold as a unit with the lot to which it is affixed. As a conveyance of real property in such a situation, a mobile-home sale no longer applies under Chapter 218 of the Wisconsin Statutes; in this situation, a real estate license would be needed.

QUESTIONS

1. A listing contract in Wisconsin must

   1. be oral.
   2. be written.
   3. name the salesperson involved.
   4. be signed by the owner of the property being listed.

2. A broker is entitled to a commission when he or she

   1. brings an offer to the seller.
   2. lists the property with a multiple-listing service.
   3. makes a good faith effort to sell the property.
   4. produces a ready, willing and able buyer.

3. Which of the following statements does not correctly describe the independent contractor relationship in Wisconsin?

   1. The independent contractor must work exclusively for the real estate company.
   2. The independent contractor is compensated on a commission basis.
   3. The independent contractor is an employee of the real estate company.
   4. The contract may be terminated at any time by either party upon notice.

4. Which of the following statements does not correctly describe the broker's responsibility for his or her own statements?

    1. A broker should not knowingly make a false representation.
    2. A broker should not make a statement of opinion without disclosing all facts known to him or her that may affect that statement.
    3. A broker may not disclose the racial characteristics of a neighborhood to a potential buyer.
    4. A broker may disclose the existence of a neighborhood group home for the handicapped to a potential buyer.

5. A broker is showing a house in which the previous owner committed suicide. The potential buyer asks whether the house has any stigma attached to it. The broker should

    1. reveal to the potential buyer that the owner committed suicide.
    2. reveal to the potential buyer that the house is stigmatized, but that by law he is not allowed to reveal the nature of the stigma.
    3. not disclose the owner's suicide to the potential buyer.
    4. tell the potential buyer that the owner committed suicide, but it is not important because it had no effect on the physical condition of the house.

6. A salesperson is conducting an open house when a couple comes through and asks questions about the physical condition of the house. The salesperson is aware that the seller had a qualified third party provide a report on the physical condition of the house. The salesperson should not

    1. disclose any information that contradicts the written report.
    2. disclose information on the physical condition of the house if the written report is available.
    3. reveal the existence of the written report.
    4. discuss the physical condition except for the major problems.

7. According to Wisconsin Statutes Chapter 709, a completed real estate condition report must be given to a buyer no later than

    1. three days prior to the acceptance of the offer to purchase.
    2. two days after the acceptance of the offer to purchase.
    3. five days after the acceptance of the offer to purchase.
    4. ten days after the acceptance of the offer to purchase.

8. If a real estate condition report required by Wisconsin Statute Chapter 709 discloses a serious defect that was not already known to a buyer prior to accepting an offer to purchase, the buyer has how many hours to rescind the offer?

    1. 24   3. 72
    2. 48   4. 108

9. The Wisconsin Statute Chapter 709 Seller Disclosure Law covers all but which of the following types of property?

    1. An owner-occupied single-family home
    2. An eight-unit apartment building
    3. A duplex
    4. A four-unit apartment building

10. The new broker agency law requires that a broker give a written agency disclosure form to

    1. just her clients.
    2. just her customers.
    3. all of her clients and customers.
    4. neither her clients nor her customers.

5

Listing Agreements

THE LISTING CONTRACT

The Wisconsin Statute of Frauds stipulates that in order for a listing to be valid it must: (1) be *in writing*, (2) state the *rate or exact amount of commission* to be earned by the broker, (3) specify a *definite termination date* for the agreement, (4) state the *price* of the real estate and the *terms of the sale*, (5) include a *description specifically identifying* the property, (6) name the *broker* and (7) bear the *signature* of the person who is to pay the broker's commission. Under the Statute of Frauds, an oral listing agreement is *unenforceable*; Wisconsin courts have been reluctant to enforce any oral listing agreements.

Types of Listings

Wisconsin brokers may use the open, exclusive agency and exclusive-right-to-sell forms of listing agreements. However, the approved exclusive-right-to-sell form would have to be modified to accommodate the first two types. Real estate *licensees are prohibited from using net listings* (Wis. Code RL24.10). A new WB-1 Residential Listing Contract was approved by Wisconsin Department of Regulation and Licensing and required for use by licensees as of February 1994.

In general, the exclusive-right-to-sell listing provides the greatest advantage for both broker and property owner. If brokers are assured of fair compensation, they can justify expending time and money on a property. When they control the sale, they can afford to advertise the property extensively and spend the necessary time on it. The owner or seller who gives an exclusive-right-to-sell listing has the right to demand the broker's preferred attention to the property. For this reason, brokers should not take such a listing unless they believe the property can be sold and intend to give it preferred attention. The new exclusive-right-to-sell contract appears on pages 9 and 10 of this chapter.

Override Clauses

In Wisconsin, an *override clause* is included in a listing agreement in order to protect the broker's commission. The override clause provides that a broker is entitled to a commission if the property is sold or exchanged within 12 months after the listing expires to anyone with whom the seller, broker or any of the broker's agents negotiated during the life of the contract and whose name(s) the broker submitted in writing to the seller not later than 3 days after the expiration of the contract. A written offer to purchase submitted to the seller during the term of the listing also will constitute such notice. The override clause is effective for 12 months in all approved listing contracts.

This material supplements Chapter 5 in *Modern Real Estate Practice* by Galaty, Allaway and Kyle.

Figure 5.1 Residential Listing Contract—Exclusive Right To Sell

Approved by Wisconsin Department of Regulation and Licensing
11-1-93 (Optional Use Date)
2-1-94 (Mandatory Use Date)

Wisconsin Legal Blank Co., Inc.
Milwaukee, Wisconsin

WB-1 RESIDENTIAL LISTING CONTRACT-EXCLUSIVE RIGHT TO SELL

1 SELLER GIVES BROKER THE EXCLUSIVE RIGHT TO SELL THE PROPERTY DESCRIBED BELOW ON THE TERMS SET FORTH IN THIS LISTING.

2 ■ **PROPERTY DESCRIPTION:** Street address is: 1400 Regas

3 in the City of Madison , County of Dane , Wisconsin.

4 (Additional description, if any:) Lot 2, Block 4, Fairmont Subdivision, NW¼ of Section B, T9N, R7E

5 Dane County, Wisconsin

6 ■ **TERMS OF LISTING:**

7 LIST PRICE: Fifty-Six Thousand Nine Hundred and 00/100--------------Dollars ($ 56,900.00).

8 TERMS: Cash or equivalent at closing or Buyer may assume seller's existing mortgage

9 OCCUPANCY DATE: Closing OCCUPANCY CHARGE: (If Seller occupies after closing): $ 25.00 per day or part thereof.

10 PROPERTY INCLUDED IN LIST PRICE: Seller agrees to include in the list price all fixtures as defined at lines 137 to 143, unless excluded at lines 15 to 17. *CAUTION:*

11 *Exclude fixtures not owned by Seller such as rented water softeners. The terms of the Offer to Purchase will determine what property is included or excluded.*

12 ADDITIONAL ITEMS INCLUDED IN THE LIST PRICE: All carpeting, drapes and drapery rods, washer, dryer,

13 and refrigerator

14

15 ITEMS NOT INCLUDED IN THE LIST PRICE: Sellers' personal property

16

17

18 ■ **CONDITION OF TITLE:** Upon payment of the purchase price, Seller shall convey the Property by warranty deed (or other conveyance as provided

19 herein) free and clear of all liens and encumbrances, except: municipal and zoning ordinances and agreements entered under them, recorded easements for

20 the distribution of utility and municipal services, recorded building and use restrictions and covenants, general taxes levied in the year of closing and

21 (provided none of the foregoing prohibit present use of the Property).

22 ■ **TITLE EVIDENCE:** Seller shall provide evidence of the condition of Seller's title in the form agreed to by buyer and Seller in the offer to purchase.

23 ■ **MARKETING:** In consideration for Seller's agreements herein Broker agrees to use reasonable efforts to procure a purchaser for the Property, including

24 but not limited to the following: Holding at least one open house, use MLS, sign in yard, newspaper

25 advertising as necessary . Seller agrees that Broker may market other properties during the term of this Listing.

26 SEE LINES 84 TO 94 REGARDING SELLER'S DUTY TO NOTIFY BROKER OF ANY POTENTIAL PURCHASER OF WHICH SELLER HAS KNOWLEDGE,

27 SELLER'S DUTY TO COOPERATE WITH BROKER'S MARKETING EFFORTS AND PROVISIONS REGARDING BROKER'S ROLE AS MARKETING AGENT.

28 ■ **OTHER BROKERS:** The parties agree that Broker will work and cooperate with other brokers in marketing the Property, including brokers from other firms

29 acting as subagents (agents of seller retained by Broker) and brokers representing buyers, except:

30 ■ **DUAL AGENCY:** If Broker represents a prospective purchaser of the Property through a buyer agency contract, Seller (does)(does not) [STRIKE ONE]

31 consent to the dual agency relationship described (at lines 148 to 155)(in the dual agency provisions of the attached addendum) [STRIKE ONE].

32 ■ **COMMISSION:** Seller shall pay Broker's commission, which shall be earned if, during the term of this Listing:

33 1) Seller accepts an offer which creates an enforceable contract for the sale of all or any part of the Property;

34 2) Seller grants an option to purchase all or any part of the Property which is subsequently exercised;

35 3) Seller enters into a binding exchange agreement on all or any part of the Property; or

36 4) A purchaser is procured for the Property by the Broker, by Seller, or by any other person, at the price and on substantially the terms set forth in

37 this Listing and the standard provisions of the current WB-11 RESIDENTIAL OFFER TO PURCHASE, even if Seller does not accept this

38 purchaser's offer. See lines 156 to 158 regarding procurement.

39 Broker's commission shall be 7 % or whichever is greater. The

40 percentage commission, if applicable, shall be calculated based on the sale price if commission is earned under 1) or 2) above, or calculated based on the list

41 price if the commission is earned on an exchange of the entire property under 3) or under 4). If less than the entire property is exchanged, the percentage

42 commission shall be calculated on the fair market value of the property exchanged. Once earned, Broker's commission is due and payable in full at the earlier

43 of closing or the date set for closing, unless otherwise agreed in writing. SHOULD LITIGATION ARISE BETWEEN THE PARTIES IN CONNECTION WITH

44 THIS LISTING, THE PREVAILING PARTY SHALL HAVE THE RIGHT TO REASONABLE ATTORNEY FEES.

45 ■ **EXCLUSIONS:** All persons whose purchase, exchange or exercise of grant of option would earn a prior listing broker a commission under a prior listing

46 contract are excluded from this Listing to the extent of the prior broker's legal rights, unless otherwise agreed to in writing. Within one week of this Listing

47 Seller agrees to deliver to Broker a list of all persons whose procurement as purchaser would earn another broker a commission under a prior listing

48 contract. *CAUTION: Contact previous listing broker if the identity of potential protected buyers from previous listings is uncertain.* Other buyers excluded

49 from this Listing until [INSERT DATE] are: None .

50 ■ **SELLER REPRESENTATIONS REGARDING PROPERTY CONDITIONS:** Seller represents to Broker that as of the date of this Listing, Seller has no

51 notice or knowledge of any conditions affecting the Property or transaction (as defined at lines 116 to 136) other than those identified in the attached real

52 estate condition report (see lines 95 to 99 regarding real estate condition reports) dated and None

53

54 *WARNING: IF SELLER REPRESENTATIONS ARE NOT CORRECT, SELLER MAY BE LIABLE FOR DAMAGES AND COSTS.*

55 ■ **TERM OF THE CONTRACT:** FROM THE 13th DAY OF September , 19 94

56 UP TO AND INCLUDING MIDNIGHT OF THE 13th DAY OF January , 19 95

57 ■ **EXTENSION OF LISTING:** This Listing may be extended by agreement of the Parties. The Listing term is extended for a period of one year as to any

58 buyer who personally or through any person acting for such buyer either negotiated or submitted a written offer to acquire an interest in the Property or

59 purchase, exchange or option during the term of this Listing. If the extension is based on negotiation, the extension shall only be effective if the buyer's name

60 is delivered to Seller, in writing, no later than three days after the expiration of the Listing, unless Seller was directly involved in the negotiations. "Negotiated"

61 for the purpose of this paragraph means to discuss the potential terms upon which buyer might acquire an interest in the Property or to attend an individual

62 showing of the Property. Upon notice that the Property has been listed with another broker during the extension period, Broker agrees to promptly deliver to

63 Seller a written list of those buyers known by Broker to whom the extension period applies.

64 ■ **ADDITIONAL PROVISIONS:** Buyer may assume seller's home insurance policy

65

66

67

68 ■ **ADDENDA:** The attached is/are made part of this Listing.

69 *CAUTION: REVIEW LINES 80 TO 158 (OVER) WHICH ARE A PART OF THIS LISTING. IF SIGNED, THIS LISTING CAN CREATE A LEGALLY*

70 *ENFORCEABLE CONTRACT. BROKERS MAY PROVIDE A GENERAL EXPLANATION OF THE PROVISIONS OF THE LISTING BUT ARE PROHIBITED*

71 *BY LAW FROM GIVING ADVICE OR OPINIONS CONCERNING YOUR LEGAL RIGHTS UNDER THIS LISTING. AN ATTORNEY SHOULD BE*

72 *CONSULTED IF LEGAL ADVICE IS NEEDED.*

73 Dated this 13th day of September , 19 94

74 (X)

75 Agent for Broker▲ (Print Name) ► John James

76 New House Realty

77 Broker/Firm▲

78 5 Royal Street, Madison (608) 275-4600

79 Broker's Address and Phone #▲ Fax # ►

74 (X)

75 Seller▲ (Print Name) ► George Carter

76 (X)

77 Seller▲ (Print Name) ► Martha Carter

78 1400 Regas Lane, Madison (608) 238-6476

79 Seller's Address and Phone #▲ Fax # ►

Figure 5.1 Residential Listing Contract—Exclusive Right To Sell (continued)

FAIR HOUSING

80 SELLER AND BROKER AGREE THAT THEY WILL NOT DISCRIMINATE AGAINST ANY PROSPECTIVE PURCHASER ON
81 ACCOUNT OF RACE, COLOR, SEX, SEXUAL ORIENTATION AS DEFINED IN WISCONSIN STATUTES, SECTION 111.32(13M), DISABILITY,
82 RELIGION, NATIONAL ORIGIN, MARITAL STATUS, LAWFUL SOURCE OF INCOME, AGE, ANCESTRY, FAMILIAL STATUS, OR IN ANY OTHER
83 UNLAWFUL MANNER.

BROKER'S ROLE AS MARKETING AGENT

84 Seller and Broker acknowledge that Broker is required to be knowledgeable regarding laws, public policies
85 and current market conditions affecting real estate and to assist, guide and advise the buying and selling public on these matters. *NOTE: WISCONSIN*
86 *LICENSE LAW PROHIBITS BROKER FROM GIVING LEGAL ADVICE OR OPINIONS CONCERNING THE LEGAL RIGHTS OR OBLIGATIONS OF*
87 *PARTIES TO A TRANSACTION OR THE LEGAL EFFECT OF A SPECIFIC CONTRACT OR CONVEYANCE. AN ATTORNEY SHOULD BE CONSULTED*
88 *IF LEGAL ADVICE IS DESIRED. SELLER SHOULD CONSULT OTHER EXPERTS AS APPROPRIATE, FOR EXAMPLE, APPRAISERS, TAX ADVISORS,*
89 *OR HOME INSPECTORS IF SERVICES BEYOND BROKER'S MARKETING SERVICES ARE REQUIRED.*

SELLER COOPERATION WITH MARKETING EFFORTS

90 Seller agrees to cooperate with Broker in Broker's marketing efforts and to provide Broker with all
91 records, documents and other material in Seller's possession or control which are required in connection with the sale. Seller authorizes Broker to do those
92 acts reasonably necessary to effect a sale and Seller agrees to cooperate fully with these efforts which may include use of a multiple listing service or a key
93 lockbox system on Property. Seller shall promptly notify Broker in writing of any potential purchasers with whom Seller negotiates during the term of this
94 Listing and shall promptly refer all persons making inquiries concerning the Property to Broker.

REAL ESTATE CONDITION REPORT

95 Seller agrees to complete the real estate condition report provided by Broker to the best of Seller's ability. Seller
96 agrees to promptly amend the report to include any defects (as defined in the report) which Seller learns of after completion of the report. Seller
97 acknowledges that failure to deliver a complete and accurate report to Buyer within ten days after acceptance of an offer to purchase may provide Buyer with
98 rights to rescind that offer to purchase under Wis. Statute Chapter 709. Seller authorizes Broker to distribute the report to all interested parties and their
99 agents and to disclose all adverse material facts as required by law.

OPEN HOUSE AND SHOWING RESPONSIBILITIES

100 Seller is aware that there is a potential risk of injury, damage and/or theft involving persons attending
101 an "individual showing" or an "open house". Seller accepts responsibility for preparing the Property to minimize the likelihood of injury, damage and/or loss of
102 personal property. Seller agrees to hold Broker harmless for any losses or liability resulting from personal injury, property damage, or theft occurring during
103 "individual showings" or "open houses" other than those caused by Broker's negligence or intentional wrongdoing. **Seller acknowledges that individual showings**
104 **may be conducted by licensees other than Broker and that buyers may photograph or videotape property, unless otherwise provided for on lines 64 to 67.**

LEASED PROPERTY

105 If Property is currently leased and lease(s) will extend beyond closing, Seller shall assign Seller's rights under the lease(s) and
106 transfer all security deposits and prepaid rents thereunder to Buyer at closing. Seller acknowledges that Seller remains liable under the lease(s) unless
107 released by tenants. *CAUTION: Seller should consider obtaining an indemnification agreement from buyer for liabilities under the lease(s) unless released*
108 *by tenants.*

EARNEST MONEY

109 If Broker holds trust funds in connection with the transaction, they shall be retained by Broker in Broker's trust account. Broker may
110 refuse to hold earnest money or other trust funds. Should Broker hold the earnest money, Seller authorizes Broker to disburse the earnest money pursuant
111 to the terms of the offer to purchase, option or exchange agreement used in the transaction.
112 If the transaction fails to close and the earnest money is disbursed to Seller, then upon disbursement to Seller the earnest money shall be paid first to
113 reimburse Broker for cash advances made by Broker on behalf of Seller and one half of the balance, but not in excess of the agreed commission, shall be paid
114 to Broker as Broker's full commission in connection with said purchase transaction and the balance shall belong to Seller. This payment to Broker shall not
115 terminate this Listing Contract.

DEFINITIONS

116 CONDITIONS AFFECTING THE PROPERTY OR TRANSACTION: A "condition affecting the Property or transaction" is defined as
117 follows:
118   (a) Planned or commenced public improvements which may result in special assessments or otherwise materially affect the Property or the present use of
119   the Property;
120   (b) Government agency or court order requiring repair, alteration or correction of any existing condition;
121   (c) Structural inadequacies which if not repaired will significantly shorten the expected normal life of the Property;
122   (d) Mechanical systems inadequate for the present use of the Property;
123   (e) Conditions constituting a significant health or safety hazard for occupants of Property;
124   (f) Insect or animal infestation of the Property;
125   (g) Underground storage tanks on the Property for storage of flammable or combustible liquids including but not limited to gasoline and heating
126   oil; **NOTE: Wisconsin Administrative Code, Chapter ILHR 10 contains registration and operation rules for such underground storage tanks.**
127   (h) Any portion of the Property being in a 100 year floodplain, a wetland or shoreland zoning area under local, state or federal regulations;
128   (i) Completed or pending reassessment of the Property for property tax purposes;
129   (j) Material violations of environmental rules or other rules or agreements regulating the use of the Property;
130   (k) Construction or remodeling on Property for which required state or local permits had not been obtained;
131   (l) Any land division involving the subject Property, for which required state or local approvals had not been obtained;
132   (m) Material violation of state or local smoke dector laws; *NOTE: Smoke detectors are required on all levels of all residential properties.*
133   (n) High voltage electric (100 KV or greater) or steel natural gas transmission lines located on but not directly serving the Property;
134   (o) That a structure on the Property is designated as a historic building or that any part of Property is in a historic district;
135   (p) Other conditions or occurrences which would significantly reduce the value of the Property to a reasonable person with knowledge of the nature and
136   scope of the condition or occurrence. See lines 50 to 54.
137 FIXTURES: A "Fixture" is an item of property which is physically attached to or so closely associated with land or buildings so as to be treated as part of the
138 real estate including, without limitation, physically attached items not easily removable without damage to the premises, items specifically adapted to the
139 premises, and items customarily treated as fixtures including but not limited to all: garden bulbs; plants; shrubs and trees; screen and storm doors and
140 windows; electric lighting fixtures; window shades; curtain and traverse rods; blinds and shutters; central heating and cooling units and attached equipment;
141 water heaters and softeners; sump pumps; attached or fitted floor coverings; awnings; attached antennas; satellite dishes and component parts; garage door
142 openers and remote controls; installed security systems; central vacuum systems and accessories; in-ground sprinkler systems and component parts;
143 built-in appliances; ceiling fans; fences; storage buildings on permanent foundations and docks/piers on permanent foundations. See lines 10 to 17.
144 *CAUTION: Address rented fixtures if any, e.g. water softener, L.P. tanks, etc.*
145 DELIVERY: Unless otherwise stated, delivery of documents or written notices may be accomplished by: 1) giving the document or written notice personally
146 to the Party; 2) by depositing the document or written notice postage or fees prepaid in the U.S. Mail or a commercial delivery system addressed to the Party
147 at the Party's address on line 78; 3) by electronically transmitting the document or written notice to the Party's fax number at line 79.
148 DUAL AGENCY: If Broker represents a prospective buyer of the Property as a buyer's agent, Broker may only continue to represent both parties with the
149 written consent of each. If the dual agency relationship arises, Broker will continue to provide the marketing services agreed upon in this Listing. As a dual
150 agent, Broker will provide information and advice to both parties, but will not place the interests of either party ahead of the other. During negotiations,
151 Broker will prepare approved forms to accomplish the intent of the party making the proposal. Broker will present the proposal in an objective and unbiased
152 manner, disclosing the proposal's advantages and disadvantages. Broker shall not disclose confidential information of either party unless required by law.
153 **(NOTE: Wisconsin Administrative Code section RL 24.07 requires disclosure of adverse material facts to all interested parties.)** *CAUTION: LEGAL*
154 *COUNSEL SHOULD BE CONSULTED ABOUT QUESTIONS REGARDING THE MODIFICATIONS TO AGENCY DUTIES RESULTING FROM THIS*
155 *DUAL AGENCY AGREEMENT.* **See lines 30 and 31.**
156 PROCURE: A purchaser is procured when a valid and binding contract of sale is entered into between the Seller and the purchaser or when a ready, willing
157 and able purchaser submits a written offer at the price and on substantially the terms specified in this Listing. A purchaser is ready, willing and able when the
158 purchaser submitting the written offer has the ability to complete the purchaser's obligations under the written offer. See lines 36 to 38.

Listing Considerations

While a real estate listing is the broker's employment contract, it is also a means of securing real estate to sell. Success depends to a great extent on the quantity and quality of the real estate that a broker has available for sale. Because a broker's public image is created partly by the real estate he or she handles, many factors should be considered before accepting employment and taking a listing.

Owners' reason for selling. Have the owners been transferred to another city? Have they outgrown their present home or do they want a smaller home? Do they want a nicer home or a less expensive one? Are they selling the house as part of the property settlement in a divorce or do they just dislike the neighbors? Perhaps they do not need to sell and are simply speculating on the market to make a profit. The owners' reasons for selling will determine how anxious they are to sell. In taking a listing, a broker also may identify a prospect who is willing to trade properties or purchase a different property. Information between the seller and the listing agent should remain confidential unless the seller authorizes the agent to disclose motives for selling.

Supply and demand. How much demand is there in a given market for a specific type of property? This is important to consider when comparing a parcel of real estate with similar properties. If the supply is great and the demand is small, it may be necessary to compensate by offering the property at a reduced price or with an extra bonus in order to sell the property within a given time.

Potential. The broker also must consider the buyer appeal that one property has over another. How will the property look to prospective purchasers? Will prospective purchasers realize the property's full potential when they see it? Is it neat and clean? Does it look as nice as other properties in the neighborhood? Are there too many or too few furnishings? Will the property be accessible at reasonable times for the broker to show it to prospective purchasers? Remember the maxim that "a property well listed is half sold." The broker should seek only as many listings as he or she can handle, emphasizing the quality rather than the quantity of the merchandise.

Termination of Listing

In Wisconsin, listing contracts may be terminated by any of the methods described in the text.

ADVERTISING

The Wisconsin Real Estate Board enforces a regulation concerning the advertising of real property by real estate licensees. Brokers and salespeople always must present a true picture of property being offered for sale. A broker may not advertise any service free of charge unless the service is available without any contingencies or strings attached. For example, a broker may offer free market analysis as an inducement to encourage listings. *Blind ads are prohibited* by Wisconsin law. These regulations and other rules relating to advertising are discussed more thoroughly in Chapter 13 of this supplement.

AN EXPLANATION OF THE LISTING CONTRACT

Information contained in this chapter is provided to assist applicants as well as licensees to understand the new WB-1 residential listing contract. This chapter includes both a sample problem and a line-by-line explanation of the listing contract. These are primarily suggestions for your review and consideration. For advice in handling particular situations, you are strongly encouraged to obtain the services of an attorney.

HIGHLIGHTS OF CHANGES REFLECTED IN THE NEW WB-1 RESIDENTIAL LISTING CONTRACT

1.   A complete legal description is no longer necessarily required in all listings.

2.   The minimum earnest money provision has been eliminated.

3.   The list of fixtures has been expanded.

4.   The presence of a "negative" utility easement has been recognized (Line 133).

5.   The broker commission is due and payable in full at the closing or the date set for closing (Lines 42–43).

6.   Should litigation arise between parties in connection with the listing, the prevailing party will have the right to reasonable attorney fees (Lines 42–43).

7.   The seller and broker are cautioned to contact previous listing brokers if the identity of potential protected buyers from previous listings is uncertain (Line 48).

8.   The override clause (extension of listing) has been increased to one year and the period of time in which the override list of buyers must be delivered to the seller has been increased to three days after the expiration of the listing.

9.   The special provisions section of the previous listing contract has been changed to additional provisions on lines 64–67.

10.   The broker's role as a marketing agent is emphasized (Lines 84–89).

11.   Lines 90–94 stress ways in which the seller must cooperate with the marketing efforts of the broker.

12.   Lines 116–158 define selected terms such as "fixtures" and "delivery."

Sample Listing

John James, a salesperson from Newhouse Realty, which is a member of the local REALTORS® Multiple-Listing Service, secured a four-month exclusive-right-to-sell listing on September 13, 1994, from George and Martha Carter. The listing was for their home at 1400 Regas Lane, Madison, Wisconsin. The Carters agreed to include the refrigerator, washer, dryer, carpeting, drapes and drapery rods in the total selling price of $56,900. The Carters will give occupancy on the date of closing. James has agreed to hold at least one open house and to list the property with a multiple-listing service.

First Federal Bank of Madison holds a mortgage on the Carters' property with an unpaid balance of $26,650 as of September 1. The monthly payment including interest is $275.10, interest is charged at the rate of 8 percent per annum and the final payment is to be made within 13 years. The bank has indicated that this mortgage may be assumed by a qualified buyer at the same rate of interest. The buyers may assume the Carters' home insurance policy from Celtic Insurance Company, which runs from May 1, 1993, to April 30, 1996, at a cost of $390.

Line-by-Line Explanation of the New WB-1 Residential Listing Contract

Line 1 indicates this is an exclusive-right-to-sell listing that protects the broker's commission even if the property is in fact sold by the owner or any other person during the term of the listing contract, provided the listing broker has made a bonafide and continuing effort to sell the property.

Lines 2–5 describe the real estate involved. A street address may be an adequate description if it identifies the property being sold. Where the street address is not an adequate description, a complete legal description should be included on these lines.

Line 6 introduces the section that will cover the terms of the listing (Lines 7–17).

Lines 7–8 show the listing price of the property as well as the terms under which the property will be sold.

Line 9 indicates the date of occupancy and use and occupancy charges if the sellers occupy after closing. The occupancy charge is a sum of money that the seller agrees to pay to the buyer each day after the specified occupancy date in which the seller fails to give occupancy to the buyer.

Lines 10–17 identify what property will be included in the list price.

Line 10 makes reference to a definition of fixtures as well as a list of fixtures present on lines 137–143.

Line 11 reminds the broker to exclude fixtures not owned by the seller such as a rental water softener and stresses that the terms of the offer to purchase will determine what property is included or excluded.

Lines 12–14 relate to any extras that may or may not be included in the property to be sold. The broker must know about the extras when talking to prospective purchasers and when drafting an offer to purchase for the property. The broker should state any items that are excluded from the sale on lines 15–17. If any of these items are included in lines 137 to 143, they should be crossed out.

If the transaction includes extras that are not fixtures but are personal property, the extras should be transferred at the time of closing by bill of sale, for they would not be covered by a normal deed or land contract. Transfer of personal property becomes particularly important in a farm transaction, when stocks, supplies and machinery often will be sold along with the real estate.

Lines 18–21 state that upon payment of the purchase price, the seller will convey the property free and clear of all liens and encumbrances except those listed on lines 19–21.

Line 22 states that the seller must provide title evidence consistent with the type specified in the offer to purchase.

Lines 23-27 relate to the efforts to be made by the broker to procure a purchaser of the property. The broker in the sample listing agreed to hold at least one open house. It is essential that the broker include in this section any agreements of what will be done.

Line 25 states that the seller agrees that the broker may market other properties during the term of the listing; a seller cannot sue a listing broker for taking a buyer to other comparable listings subsequent to showing the seller's property.

Lines 26–27 make reference to lines 84–94 that describe the broker's role as marketing agent, as well as the seller's responsibility to cooperate with the broker's marketing efforts and notify the broker of any potential purchaser of which the seller has knowledge.

Lines 28–29 provide that the seller agrees that the broker will cooperate with other brokers, including subagents and brokers representing the buyers. Chapter RL 24.13(2)(a) specifies that the listing brokers shall permit all buyers and their agents access to the listed property for showing unless such access is contrary to the seller's specific written instructions. If the seller wishes to limit the agreement in some way, these limitations would be placed on line 29.

Lines 30–31 state that if a broker represents a prospective buyer of the property through a buyer agency contract, the seller may accept or reject the dual agency relationship described at lines 148–155. Lines 30–31 also offer the broker the right to use the dual agency disclosure information on lines 148–155 or draft his or her own dual agency provision. Brokers drafting their own provisions should have them reviewed by an attorney.

Lines 32–44 refer to the percentage of commission to be charged by the broker. Section 240.10 of the Wisconsin Statutes requires that the listing contract specify the commission to be paid. The listing usually will provide for a commission based on a percentage of the total price for which the property is sold. It is important to note that lines 36–38 state that if a purchaser is procured for the property by the broker, seller or by any other person, at the price and on substantially the terms identified in the listing and the standard provision of the offer to purchase, the broker will have earned the commission. The broker will have earned the commission even if the seller refuses to accept the buyer's offer. The term "procure" is defined on lines 156–158.

Line 41 covers a situation in which less than the entire property is exchanged; it states that the percentage commission shall be based on the fair market value of the property exchanged.

Line 42 states that the broker's commission, once earned, will be due and payable in full at the earlier of closing or the date set for closing, unless otherwise agreed in writing.

Lines 43–44 provide that if litigation arises between the parties in connection with the listing, the prevailing party will have the right to reasonable attorney fees. If a broker wins a commission lawsuit, he or she will be able to recover attorney fees that were not provided for in previous listing contracts. If the broker loses the lawsuit, he or she will have to pay the attorney fees of the seller.

Lines 45–49 are used to list the names of those people with whom the sellers have been dealing on their own and whom the sellers consider as potential purchasers and want to be excluded from the contract; line 49 includes a blank for inserting a date if the seller's exceptions are to end before the listing expires. The sellers list must be provided within one week of the listing. The new listing contract cautions the broker and the seller to contact any previous broker if the identity of protected buyers is uncertain; all buyers under a previous listing contract are automatically excluded unless otherwise agreed to in writing.

Lines 50–54 cover information provided to the broker by the seller as identified in the attached real estate condition report; lines 95–99 explain the significance of the real estate condition report that is discussed in Chapter 4 of this book.

Line 50 makes clear that the seller's representations are effective as of the date of the listing. The conditions affecting the property or transaction are defined at lines 116–136. For example, line 120 requires the seller to make a representation as to whether he or she is aware of any government agency or court order requiring repair, alterations or correction of any existing condition.

Lines 57–63 provide information on the extension of the listing; it may be extended by agreement of the parties.

Lines 57–60 extend the listing for <u>one year</u> for any buyer who personally or through any person acting for the buyer either negotiated to acquire an interest in the property or submitted a written offer to purchase, exchange or option during the term of the listing. The extension is only effective if the buyer's name is delivered to the seller, in writing, no later than <u>three days</u> after the expiration of the listing, unless the seller was directly involved in the negotiation.

Lines 60–62 state that "negotiated" means to discuss the potential terms upon which a buyer might acquire an interest in the property or to attend an individual showing of the property.

Lines 62–63 also state that upon notice that the property has been listed with another broker during the extension period, the broker agrees to promptly deliver to the seller a written list of those buyers known by the broker to whom the extension period applies.

Lines 64–67 do not have to be filled in. These lines are used for special provision such as specific requests made by the seller. For example, the sellers could indicate that they do not want buyers to photograph or videotape their house.

Line 68 allows for addenda to be made part of the listing such as an explanation of the role of a buyer broker in the transaction.

Lines 73–79 relate to signing of the listing agreement by the various parties involved.

Lines 80–83 state that the seller and broker agree not to discriminate against prospective buyers and indicates those classes protected under state law.

Lines 84–89 make clear the broker's role as a marketing agent rather than, for example, an attorney or home inspector.

Lines 90–94 identify the responsibilities of the seller in cooperating with the broker's marketing effort. For example, the seller is responsible for promptly notifying the broker in writing of any potential buyers with whom the seller negotiates during the term of the listing and promptly referring all persons making inquiries concerning the property to the broker.

Lines 95–99 state that the seller agrees to complete the real estate condition report provided by the broker to the best of the seller's ability. The seller also agrees to amend the report when he or she learns of any defects after completion of the report. This section of the listing reflects Wisconsin Statute Chapter 709. It is also important to note that the seller authorizes the broker to distribute the report to all interested parties and their agents and to disclose all material facts as required by law.

Lines 100–104 address the responsibilities of the seller in regard to open house and showing responsibilities.

On lines 101–102 the seller accepts responsibility for preparing the property to minimize the likelihood of injury, damage or loss of property during an open house or showing. This section also states that the seller agrees to hold the broker harmless for any losses or liability resulting from personal injury, damage, etc. occurring during the open house or showing other than those caused by the broker's negligence or intentional wrongdoing. This section also states that buyers may photograph or videotape the property unless the seller has indicated otherwise in lines 64–67.

Lines 105–108 cover a property that has been leased. For example, lines 105–106 state that if current leases on the property extend beyond the closing, the seller will assign all rights under the leases as well as transfer all security deposits and prepaid rents to the buyer at closing.

Lines 109–115 state that if the broker holds trust funds in connection with the transaction, they shall be retained in the broker's trust account. It is important to emphasize that the broker may refuse to hold earnest money or other trust funds.

Lines 112–115 deal with how earnest money will be shared between the seller and the broker if the transaction fails to close.

Lines 116–158 include definitions of terms used in the listing contract. Lines 118–135 identify conditions affecting the property transaction. Lines 137–144 define fixtures while delivery is defined on lines 145–147. Lines 148–155 discuss dual agency with regard to the increasing role of buyer brokers. Lines 156–158 define the term "procure."

QUESTIONS

1. The type of listing agreement that best assures the seller that the broker will give the property preferred attention and best assures the broker of receiving fair compensation is what type of listing?

   1. Open
   2. Net
   3. Exclusive agency
   4. Exclusive right to sell

2. According to the Wisconsin Statute of Frauds, a listing agreement

   1. must be in writing in order to be enforceable.
   2. must not be made for a period of longer than 60 days.
   3. need not state the price of the real estate.
   4. need not state the rate of commission.

Use the information contained in the listing contract on pages 9 and 10 to answer questions 3 through 6.

3. According to the listing contract, which of the following statements is true?

   1. The override is good for five months.
   2. The sellers prohibit prospective buyers from assuming the existing mortgage.
   3. The refrigerator is not included in the sale.
   4. The broker will receive a 7 percent commission on the sale price of the house.

4. Which of the following statements is true regarding the sellers?

   1. They will list an asking price of $26,650.
   2. They will promise to include the carpeting and the draperies as part of the sales price.
   3. They will not include the washer in the sales price.
   4. They will not allow the buyer to assume their home insurance policy.

5. The listing contract does not

   1. require the broker to hold at least one open house.
   2. expire after midnight of January 13, 1993.
   3. provide for an occupancy charge of $25 per day.
   4. require the prospective sellers to deposit $2,000 in escrow to guarantee occupancy.

6. Information on the override clause is found in which of the following lines on the listing contract?

   1. 2–12
   2. 23–25
   3. 45–49
   4. 57–63

7. A broker is preparing a listing contract for a seller of a home. The broker is explaining how the property will be marketed. This type of information would be placed in which of the following lines on a listing contract?

   1. 15–17
   2. 23–25
   3. 39–44
   4. 50–53

8. You are filling out a listing contract for a seller and have just agreed that there will be a $60 occupancy charge per day if the seller occupies the property after closing. This information should be placed in which of the following lines on the listing contract?

   1. 7
   2. 9
   3. 24–25
   4. 55–56

9. The listing contract is approved by the Wisconsin

   1. Department of Regulation and Licensing.
   2. Department of Industry, Labor and Human Relations.
   3. Real Estate Board.
   4. Department of Development.

10. If a listed property is exchanged, the commission will be based on

    1. the list price.
    2. the sales price.
    3. the average of the list price and the sales price.
    4. either the list price or the sales price, whichever is preferred by the seller.

11. The override clause in Wisconsin is good for

    1. 1 month.
    2. 3 months.
    3. 6 months.
    4. 12 months.

6

Interests in Real Estate

Estates in Land

Wisconsin recognizes freeholds in *fee simple, fee determinable, fee subject to a condition subsequent* and *life estates*, as described in Chapter 6 of the text.

Legal Life Estates

Homestead (Sections 706.01 and 766.605). Every resident of Wisconsin is entitled to claim a homestead exemption from a court sale of property to pay debts. This includes both single and married homeowners. Generally, a homeowner must claim such an exemption to be entitled to it. A homeowner who is being sued by a creditor may notify the officer making the levy that he or she is claiming a homestead exemption. Exemptions do not have to be filed before a claim is lodged. The officer involved in a levy is usually a local sheriff who officially seizes the property of a judgment debtor and holds it until the claim is settled. Failure to make this claim for a specific property at the time of levy may result in a waiver of the *right to selection of homestead.*

In Wisconsin, a homestead is specifically defined for both urban and rural dwellings. An *urban homestead* consists of the home and the lot on which it is located (including any rented space, as in the case of a duplex) and any space within the building used for commercial purposes. A *rural homestead* includes the house in which a homeowner dwells and the surrounding land necessary for the use of the dwelling as a home, but not less than one-quarter acre and not more than 40 acres.

The amount of the homestead exemption is $40,000. This does not exempt payment of mortgages, laborers' and construction liens, purchase-money liens or taxes. These kinds of debts must be satisfied from the sale proceeds before the homeowner receives the exempt portion. For example, a homeowner owes $10,000 to a judgment creditor. Sale of the homestead brings $55,000. Because the homeowner owes $5,000 on the mortgage, this amount is paid before the homestead exemption of $40,000 is applied. From the $50,000 left from the proceeds of the sale after payment of the mortgage, the first $40,000 goes to the homeowner and the remaining $10,000 is applied to the homeowner's debts. If one spouse dies, the homestead rights in any property he or she owned at the time of death go to the surviving spouse.

Dower and Curtesy

Dower and curtesy do not exist as common-law rights in Wisconsin. Prior to 1986, however, the rights of the surviving spouse, whether widow or widower, were protected by statutory dower rights. The statutes pertaining to dower prior to 1986 gave the surviving spouse rights to one-third of any property that the decedent owned at death. Under those laws, the surviving spouse was entitled to a fee-simple interest in the real estate on the death of the spouse.

This material supplements Chapter 6 in *Modern Real Estate Practice* by Galaty, Allaway and Kyle.

Prior to 1986 in Wisconsin, the surviving spouse was able to renounce dower in order to elect a share in the estate under the laws of descent and distribution. Election was the right to take one-third of the estate minus the value of any property given outright to the spouse in a will. The right to elect could be barred by the written consent of both parties before or after marriage. It also could be barred if the spouse received at least one-half of certain specific properties.

The new Wisconsin Marital Property Act, discussed in greater detail in Chapter 7, presumes that all property of spouses is marital property unless otherwise classified. The dower right to an elective share is abolished because the spouse acquires a one-half interest in all marital property. More specifically, each spouse has a present undivided one-half interest in each item of marital property. If one spouse dies, that spouse dies owning a one-half interest and the surviving spouse owns the other half. The deceased spouse's one-half interest will be probated as that spouse's estate.

Easements

An easement is a right acquired by one person to use the land owned by another person for a specific purpose. All the types of easements mentioned in the text are applicable in Wisconsin. The state purchases *conservation easements* from private landowners, including *scenic easements, hunting rights* and *the right not to have the land drained or game cover cut.* Public easements usually are acquired by a state in order to preserve the land for the enjoyment of the public and to prevent private development. Public easements usually are preserved for their aesthetic value, for their historical interest or for the preservation of wildlife. Public and private easements are becoming increasingly important encumbrances on land. Licensees are required to know of existing easements so that prospective buyers can be informed.

Easement by prescription. In Wisconsin, a person may acquire an easement by prescription in the land of another provided that he or she has had *continuous* and *uninterrupted* use of the easement for a period of *20 years.* Such use also must be *open,* so that the owner easily knows of it, and *hostile,* that is, without the owner's permission.

Water Rights

The water laws of Wisconsin are based on the *public trust doctrine* contained in the state constitution. This doctrine maintains that *all navigable waters are held in trust by the state for the public.* A stream is considered navigable if it is capable of floating the lightest boat or is used for recreation or any other purpose on a regularly recurring basis. The beds of natural lakes also are owned by the state and held in trust for the public. Owners of adjoining upland have title to the land above the ordinary high watermark and a qualified right in the exposed lakebed in front of their property. The owner of land adjoining rivers and streams owns the streambed to the center, but *the rights to use the stream are subject to regulation.* Some activities require permits from local municipalities, county zoning administrators, the U.S. Army Corps of Engineers or similar sources. In Wisconsin, the principles that relate to regulating the use of water are: (1) the *riparian right doctrine of reasonable use,* which provides that all riparians have the right to use the water adjacent to their land and (2) the *doctrine of prior appropriation,* which is used for allocating water among private users when water supplies are short.

In response to a relative shortage of water and a Wisconsin Supreme Court decision, the right of prior appropriation, as discussed in the text, has been emphasized recently in the state. The court decision held that *prior beneficial users of water,* in effect, *have a property right* and that they may refuse consent to a future irrigator if they are beneficially using the water that would be diverted. Under prior appropriation, the rights of an existing user take precedence over the rights of a person applying for use. Prior-appropriation rights have been upheld for many reasons, including the recognition by the courts that substantial investment usually is required for many uses of water, especially irrigation.

Under the pure system of prior appropriation used in many of the western states, all users of water must obtain an appropriation permit for the use of a specific quantity of water. The oldest permit in force has the superior rights, so if the water supply diminishes, the most recent permittees must cease their use in favor of the more senior users.

Wisconsin does not use a pure prior-appropriation system, *but under Wisconsin's system, consent is required from an existing user before a new permit can be issued.* The relative rights of existing permittees are looked into only when complaints are received. After a hearing, a junior user might be required to modify his or her use of water to protect the rights of a senior user. *In all cases, however, the public right to use water prevails over private rights.*

The Wisconsin Department of Natural Resources (DNR) regulates water use in the state. The department determines the amount of surplus water available and when water diversions must cease. The DNR may revoke most permits if the diversion of waters is found to be harmful to a lake or stream or to other riparians.

QUESTIONS

1. Faced with a court sale of the family home to satisfy debts, a homeowner may claim a homestead exemption against

   1. real estate taxes.
   2. a mortgage loan.
   3. general creditors.
   4. a construction lien.

2. The homestead exemption from claims of unsecured creditors granted by Wisconsin law to a homeowner is

   1. $40,000.
   2. $25,000.
   3. $10,000.
   4. 5 percent of the property's market value.

3. In Wisconsin, a person may claim an easement by prescription to the land of another if he or she

   1. lived secretly on the land for 20 years.
   2. lived on the land openly for 14 years.
   3. had continuous, open and hostile use of the land for 20 years.
   4. lived on the land openly for 10 years.

4. Which of the following statements does not correctly describe the water laws of Wisconsin?

   1. Wisconsin water laws are based on the public trust doctrine.
   2. All navigable waters are held in trust by the state for the public.
   3. Wisconsin uses a prior-appropriation system.
   4. The public right to use water always prevails over private rights.

5. Which of the following statements does not correctly describe the impact of the Wisconsin Marital Property Act on the rights of the spouse?

   1. All property of the spouses is presumed to be marital property unless otherwise classified.
   2. The dower right to an elective share is abolished.
   3. Each spouse acquires a one-third interest in all marital property.
   4. Each spouse has a present undivided one-half interest in each item of marital property.

6. The amount of land for a rural homestead in Wisconsin is defined as not less than one-quarter acre and not more than how many acres?

   1. 10   3. 40
   2. 20   4. 160

7

How Ownership Is Held

FORMS OF OWNERSHIP

Wisconsin recognizes the three forms of ownership that are described in Chapter 7 of the text: *ownership in severalty, co-ownership (joint tenancy and tenancy in common)* and *ownership in trust*. The new Wisconsin Marital Property Act creates new forms of ownership that are similar to community property, as will be discussed in this chapter.

Co-Ownership

Under the new Marital Property Act, all property is presumed to be marital property unless another classification, such as individual property, is established. Tenancy by the entirety has been abolished in Wisconsin. A conveyance to two persons who are not married automatically creates a tenancy in common, unless the deed expressly states the intention to create a joint tenancy.

Partition. Any joint tenant, tenant in common or spouse under the Marital Property Act may file a *suit for partition*. If the land involved cannot be partitioned or divided fairly among the co-owners, the court may order the property sold and the proceeds distributed to the former co-owners.

The Wisconsin Marital Property Act (Section 766)

The Wisconsin Marital Property Act became effective January 1, 1986. Wisconsin is the first state in the country to adopt a version of the Uniform Marital Property Act written by a group of legal scholars. The new law creates a different property law system for married people. The new system is based on the assumption that property acquired during a marriage belongs equally to both partners. The law legally recognizes the family as an economic unit and the equal value of the contribution made by each spouse to the family, whether the contribution is money or services or both.

The act shifts Wisconsin from a common-law property system to a community property system. Under the common-law property system, each spouse owns the property he or she earns, inherits or is given. Under the community property system, the wife and husband are considered as one economic unit and share equally in most assets and debts during the marriage.

Under the Marital Property Act, all property acquired by spouses during a marriage and after January 1, 1986, is classified as either marital property or individual property. All property of spouses is marital property except as otherwise classified by the act, and all property is presumed to be marital property. Each spouse has a present undivided one-half interest in each item of marital property.

The presumption of marital property means that a person wishing to maintain individual ownership of an asset is responsible for proving its individual classification. Unless it can be proved otherwise,

---

This material supplements Chapter 7 in *Modern Real Estate Practice* by Galaty, Allaway and Kyle.

the asset is classified as marital property. With the exception of its income, property brought to the marriage at its beginning by one spouse, or property later inherited by or given to that spouse alone, is classified as individual property.

The new law applies only to property acquired by spouses after January 1, 1986. Property already owned by married persons prior to the act's effective date is not classified. If individual property is mixed with marital property, it will become marital property unless the individual property can be traced. Property acquired during the marriage before the determination date is deferred marital property if still owned by the spouse at the date of death, if the property would have been marital property if acquired after the determination date. The Marital Property Act affects spouses whenever the determination date applies. The determination date is the date on which the new marital property law becomes effective for spouses. The Marital Property Act applies to spouses when the *last* of the following occurs:

1.   January 1, 1986;

2.   the date on which a Wisconsin couple is married; or

3.   the date on which spouses establish a marital residence in Wisconsin.

Deferred marital property will be treated in probate as marital property.

The Marital Property Act also permits all spouses to title property as survivorship marital property. This new form of title is similar to joint tenancy in that the property goes to the surviving spouse without probate when one spouse dies. Moreover, if spouses acquire property after January 1, 1986, and title the property in joint tenancy, the property becomes survivorship marital property. If the spouses title the property as tenancy in common, the property becomes marital property. If the spouses purchase real estate after January 1, 1986, and use it as their personal home, the real estate will be presumed to be survivorship marital property unless the deed or document of transfer indicates a contrary intent.

In summary, the law establishes the following classifications of property:

1.   **Marital Property**—property owned equally by both spouses, such as income from a paycheck or interest on an investment.

2.   **Individual Property**—property owned by one spouse alone that was either owned prior to January 1, 1986, or marriage or received during marriage as a gift or an inheritance.

3.   **Mixed Property**—the mixing of marital property and individual property results in all of the property being presumed to be marital property. Spouses desiring to preserve individual property will have to keep detailed records so that the part of mixed property that is individual property can be traced. An example of mixed property would be a savings account begun with individual funds that becomes mixed as interest accumulates on the account.

4.   **Survivorship Marital Property**—marital property that goes directly to the surviving spouse without probate; it is similar to property owned as joint tenants.

5.   **Deferred Marital Property**—property acquired by a spouse during marriage, but before the effective date of the law for the couple, that would have been marital property if acquired after the effective date. The surviving spouse may elect to receive up to one-half of the deferred marital property on the death of the acquiring spouse. The other one-half is distributed under the deceased spouse's will.

The Marital Property Act also permits spouses to hold property in any form permitted by other laws, including a concurrent form and a form that provides the incident of survivorship ownership. Examples of these forms of property ownership are tenancy in common and joint tenancy, respectively. If, after January 1, 1986, an effort is made to establish a joint tenancy exclusively between spouses, the Marital Property Act classifies that property as survivorship marital property (an exception is made when the property is given to the spouses by a third person in the form of a joint tenancy). The Wisconsin Marital Property Act expressly authorizes spouses to enter into marital property agreements to alter many of the new property ownership rules.

Condominiums (Section 703)

Wisconsin law permits ownership of condominium units. Legally, they are called *unit ownerships.* The unit owner's interest is like any other fee simple because it may be sold and, upon the owner's death, the interest passes to his or her heirs unless disposed of by a will. In certain areas of Wisconsin, unit owners also may rent out or lease their units for a limited period.

The current Condominium Statute, *Chapter 703 of the Wisconsin Statutes*, replaced the prior condominium law in Wisconsin, which had been established in 1963. The current statute, also known as the *Condominium Ownership Act,* became effective on August 1, 1978. Included among the provisions of Chapter 703 are various consumer-protection requirements regarding disclosures, conversions, "sweetheart" contracts and declarant control. For example, S.703.33 requires that the *declarant of a residential condominium provide a prospectus to interested purchasers* of units. These disclosure materials must be *delivered not later than 15 days prior to the closing* and must contain copies of the condominium documents, contracts, leases and budgets, all in a prescribed format. The act further specifies in S.703.33(2) that conspicuous disclosure statements must be printed on the cover of the materials. In addition, S.703.33(4) states that a prospective purchaser is entitled to rescind his or her contract of sale at any time within five business days following receipt of the disclosure materials or changes thereto.

Condominium conversion is another area in which consumer-protection requirements are addressed in the current condominium law, although the *provisions on conversion apply only to residential properties*. S.703.08 provides that the property may not be converted without prior written notice to existing tenants. The tenants are given an exclusive option to purchase a unit for 60 days following the delivery of the notice. Furthermore, the tenants must be given 120 days' advance written notice of the proposed conversion. Thus, existing tenants are allowed a period of time to relocate and acquire new accommodations if they elect not to purchase a unit in the converted condominium pursuant to the notice. The tenants may not be required to vacate the property during the 120-day notice period except for violation of the lease or nonpayment of rent.

S.703.35 grants the unit owners the right to terminate sweetheart contracts and leases entered into by the declarant on behalf of the association. *Sweetheart contracts* are contracts with affiliates of the declarant or contracts that are advantageous or remunerative for the declarant rather than in the best interests of the association. S.703.35 states that any contract with the declarant or affiliates of the declarant, any contract or lease that is not bona fide or reasonable and other specified contracts and leases entered into before the association officers are elected by unit owners *may be terminated* by the association at any time without penalty on *90 days' notice.*

The consumer orientation of the current condominium law also is apparent in the manner in which declarant control is treated. The declarant is permitted only limited control of an association subject to restrictions. For example, S.703.15(2)(c) states that a declarant may not control an association for more than 3 years (10 years in the case of an expandable condominium) or 30 days after the sale of 75 percent of the common-element interest. In addition, S.703.15(2)(d) specifies that the unit owners (other than declarant) are entitled to elect directors to the Board of the Association as sales of units progress (25 percent of the directors prior to the sale of 25 percent of the common-element interest and one-third of the directors prior to the sale of 50 percent of the common-element interest). The creation, ownership, operation and administration of condominiums also are described in Chapter 7 of the text.

Partnerships

Both the *Uniform Partnership Act* and the *Uniform Limited Partnership Act* have been adopted to regulate partnerships in Wisconsin.

Land Trusts

Land trusts, as described in the text, are permitted in Wisconsin provided that the terms of the trust agreement and the powers of the trustee are stated clearly and specifically.

QUESTIONS

1. A deed grants title to a parcel of real estate "to Jane and Lisa Pascale." Lisa and Jane will acquire title to the parcel as

   1. owners in severalty.
   2. tenants in common.
   3. owners in trust.
   4. joint tenants.

2. A conveyance to two persons who are husband and wife automatically creates a/an

   1. tenancy in common.
   2. marital property.
   3. tenancy by the entirety.
   4. ownership in severalty.

3. Wisconsin law permits ownership of condominiums that are legally described as

   1. time shares.
   2. unit ownerships.
   3. cooperatives.
   4. planned unit developments.

4. Under the Marital Property Act, all property acquired by spouses during a marriage and after January 1, 1986, is classified as what type of property?

   1. Individual
   2. Marital
   3. Separate
   4. Community

5. Which of the following types of property would not be a classification of property under the Marital Property Act?

   1. Marital
   2. Separate
   3. Deferred marital
   4. Mixed

6. Harry and Rita Worth were married in Illinois on December 1, 1985, and moved to Wisconsin and established a marital residence on February 1, 1986. The date on which the Marital Property Act becomes effective for Harry and Rita is

   1. December 1, 1985.
   2. January 1, 1986.
   3. February 1, 1986.
   4. March 1, 1986.

7. According to Wisconsin law, the declarant of a residential condominium must provide a prospectus to interested purchasers of units not later than how many days prior to the closing?

   1. 3
   2. 5
   3. 15
   4. 30

8. You are a prospective purchaser of a condominium and you have just received disclosure materials from the declarant of the condominium development. You are entitled to rescind your contract of sale at any time within the next

   1. 5 business days.
   2. 10 business days.
   3. 30 business days.
   4. 45 business days.

8

Legal Descriptions

Legal Descriptions

In Wisconsin, land may be identified by *rectangular survey* or by the *subdivision lot and block* as stipulated in a recorded plat. Both of these methods are acceptable as legal descriptions. Description by *metes and bounds* also may be used in connection with either the rectangular survey or the lot-and-block method. These methods are discussed further in Chapter 8 of the text.

A legal description of the property must be included in deeds, land contracts, mortgages or other instruments to be recorded in the register of deeds office. A street address alone is not an acceptable legal description because it does not by itself accurately describe the boundaries of the property. An example of an acceptable legal description in Wisconsin is:

Lot 2, Block 4, Fairmont Subdivision, NW ¼ of Section 8, Township 9
North, Range 7 East, Dane County, Wisconsin.

Rectangular survey. Rectangular survey descriptions are determined from *the Fourth Principal Meridian and baseline*. The Fourth Principal Meridian is a north-south line that runs about 50 miles west of Madison, while the baseline is the southern boundary of the state. The map on page 25 illustrates the numbering of townships in Wisconsin and shows the baseline and meridian.

Plats. Any property owner who intends to subdivide one piece of property into five or more parcels of one and one-half acres or less and offer them for sale is required by Wisconsin law to file a plat of subdivision in the public record of the county in which the property is located. An example of a plat as it may appear on the licensing examination is shown on page 26.

This material supplements Chapter 8 in *Modern Real Estate Practice* by Galaty, Allaway and Kyle.

Figure 8.1   Wisconsin Townships Map

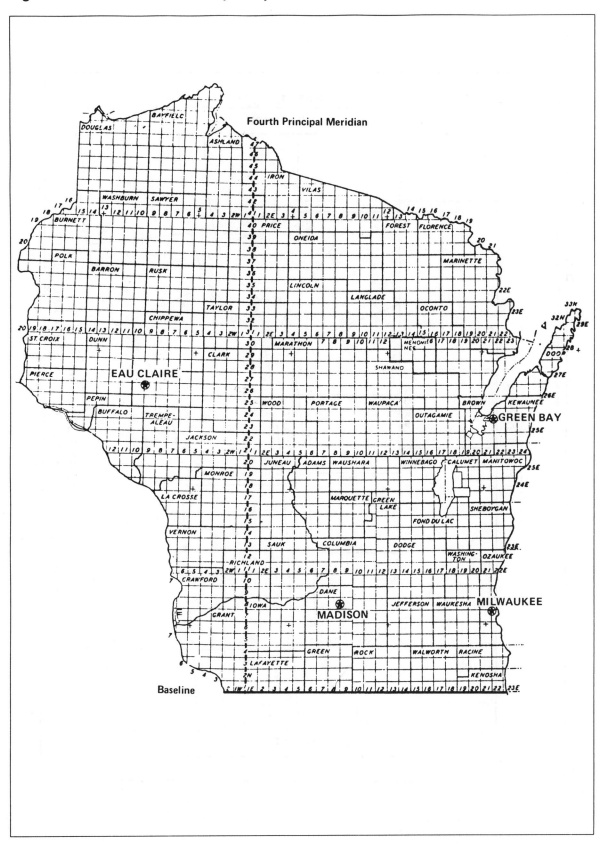

Figure 8.2   Plat of Grassland Acres Estates Subdivision Map

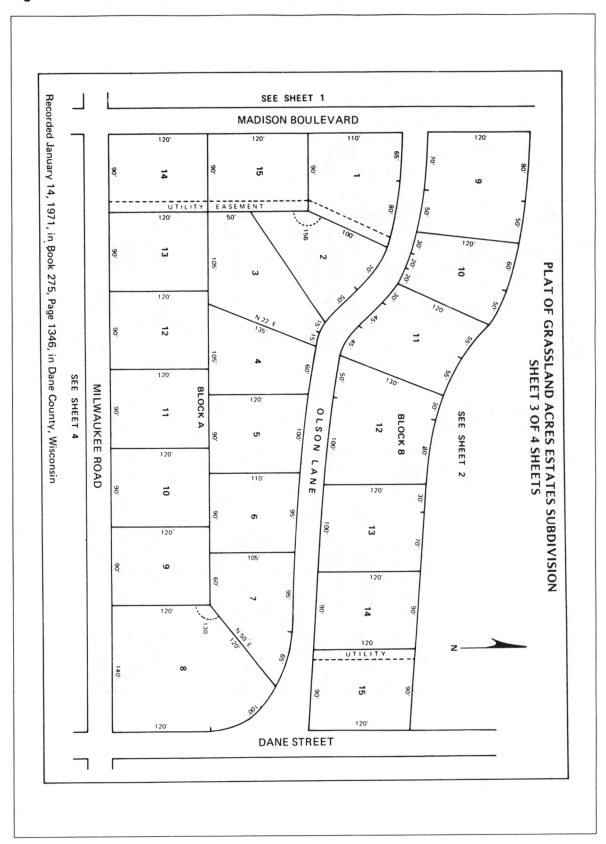

QUESTIONS

1. Which of the following does *not* constitute a proper legal description of a parcel of real estate in Wisconsin?

    1. Identification by subdivision lot and block
    2. Identification according to the rectangular-survey system
    3. Identification by metes and bounds in connection with the rectangular survey
    4. Property's street address

2. A property owner must file a plat of subdivision for record if he or she plans to divide a parcel of real estate and offer it for sale as

    1. four or more separate parcels, each two acres or less.
    2. five or more separate parcels, each one and one-half acres or less.
    3. six or more separate parcels, each one and one-half acres or less.
    4. three or more separate parcels, each one acre or less.

3. A Wisconsin property located in Township 2 North, Range 4 East, is in what county?

    1. Green   3. Grant
    2. Lafayette   4. Iowa

Use the information given on the plat of Grassland Acres Estates on page 26 to answer questions 4 through 6.

4. Which of the following statements is true?

    1. Lot 9, Block A is larger than Lot 12 in the same block.
    2. The plat for the lots on the southerly side of Milwaukee Road between Madison Boulevard and Dane Street is found on Sheet 3.
    3. Lot 9, Block A is the same size as Lot 12 in the same block.
    4. Lot 14, Block A is larger than Lot 15 in the same block.

5. Which of the following lots has the most frontage on Olson Lane?

    1. Lot 10, Block B
    2. Lot 11, Block B
    3. Lot 1, Block A
    4. Lot 2, Block A

6. Which of the following statements is true of the Wisconsin baseline?

    1. It runs about 50 miles west of Madison.
    2. It is the northern boundary of the state.
    3. It runs about 20 miles south of Madison.
    4. It is the southern boundary of the state.

9

Real Estate Taxes and Other Liens

REAL ESTATE TAX

Exemptions

In Wisconsin, as in other states, exemptions from real estate taxes are permitted for educational, religious, benevolent and charitable institutions. *Once every five years, persons claiming exemptions must submit before May 1 a prescribed form describing the use of the property for tax-exempt purposes.* Exemptions are not given to members of the armed forces, but extended payment privileges usually are permitted.

Levy and Assessment

The annual real estate tax is *levied as of January 1 for the preceding calendar year and taxes become a lien from that date.* Generally, taxes are levied on the basis of a property assessment made by the assessor for each municipality. However, taxes also may be levied on a countywide basis under a county-assessor system. This system may be established for any county if 60 percent of the members of the county board approve and pass a resolution or ordinance adopting such a system. Kenosha County is the only county in Wisconsin that currently is assessed on a county-assessor basis. Each municipality has an assessor who is in charge of the tax roll and assessments. Appraisers work under the assessor and establish the value of property in the municipality for placement on the tax roll.

The assessed valuation is usually a percentage of the market value as determined by the assessor. The specific percentage of the assessor's market determination can vary from one municipality to another. Property owners generally receive an estimate of the assessed valuation of their real estate on or about July 1 of the year of the tax; larger municipalities may mail notices at a later date. Objections to the assessed valuation may be made to the *board of review* of a municipality up to the date of the board's fifth meeting of the year.

Tax Rate

The property tax is stated as so many mills for each $1 of assessed valuation. A mill is one-tenth of a cent ($.001) and there are 1,000 mills in one dollar ($1). For example, a levy of 54.4 mills can be computed as 54.4 mills divided by 1,000, which is a tax of $.0544, or 5.44 cents per dollar.

$$\frac{54.4}{1,000} = 1,000\overline{)\begin{array}{c} .0544 \\ 54.4000 \end{array}}$$

This material supplements Chapter 9 in *Modern Real Estate Practice* by Galaty, Allaway and Kyle.

Payment

Real estate taxes in Wisconsin are paid in arrears. The taxpayer may pay the tax for the calendar year in *one payment on or before January 31 of the year following the property tax assessment.* The taxpayer has the alternative of paying *one-half* of the tax bill *on or before January 31* of the year following the levy and the *second half on or before July 31.* In Milwaukee, city real estate taxes may be paid in ten installments and county real estate taxes may be paid in seven installments. Payment is made to the treasurer of each municipality.

Delinquency

A monthly interest charge of 1 percent on the unpaid balance (computed from January 1) is added to each tax installment that is not paid by the January 31 due date. The county board or city council also may impose an additional penalty of ½ percent per month on any delinquent real estate taxes or special assessments. Property owners may redeem their property from delinquent taxes by paying all past-due taxes, penalties, interest and costs. *This redemption must be made within three years of the date of the delinquency entry* or thereafter, if the county has not entered into a contract of sale or transferred title by a county deed as a result of a tax sale.

Tax Sale

When property taxes are *past due for three years*, the county may give notice in the local newspapers and hold a *tax sale.* The county issues a deed to the property to itself, and when the property is later sold to a new owner, the county issues a deed to the new owner. No tax deed may be issued without notice to the property owner.

OTHER LIENS

Special Assessments

The procedure for special assessments outlined in Chapter 9 of the text applies to Wisconsin practice. The municipality sets up a time schedule and bills the taxpayer for an annual prorated portion of the total unpaid assessment. For example, a $1,000 charge for curb and gutter prorated over five years would be added to the annual tax bill at a rate of $200 per year. The length of the repayment period is determined by each municipality.

Mechanics' Liens

In Wisconsin, mechanics' liens are referred to as *construction liens* and may be obtained by those who furnish labor, materials or professional services in the improvement of an owner's land or buildings. Construction liens in Wisconsin take priority from the date of visible commencement of the work on an improvement or from the beginning of substantial excavation for foundation footing or base in any new construction.

Lien notice. A *prime contractor*—that is, one who deals directly with an owner—must, within *ten days* after labor has begun or materials have been furnished, give the owner written notice that any person who furnishes labor or materials has lien rights in the event that payment is not made. If payment is not made, the contractor must give the owner a warning notice that a lien is pending within five months after completing the work. The contractor also must file a lien claim with the clerk of the circuit court within six months after completing the work but no sooner than 30 days after the warning notice has been given.

A *subcontractor* or *material supplier* must (except on large projects) give the owner notice within *60 days* after first furnishing the labor or materials and must comply with the warning notice and filing requirements that apply to the prime contractor.

Action against an owner who has not made payment must begin with the filing of a summons or complaint by the contractor or subcontractor within *two years* after a claim is filed. In Wisconsin, a construction lien takes priority over an unrecorded mortgage unless notice of the mortgage is given. There is no priority among lien claimants in a foreclosure judgment.

Judgments

Judgments are effective after they are issued by a court, docketed and filed with a county recorder. They are liens within the county in which they are recorded, but they may be recorded and enforced in other counties. Where recorded, they remain liens against the properties involved for ten years. Homestead exemptions generally are effective against judgment liens up to the amount of $40,000. Judgments may be renewed and they can attach to property that is purchased after the judgment has been granted.

TAX ASSESSORS

An assessor is a public official who appraises property for tax purposes. The Wisconsin Department of Revenue certifies appraisers in the state.

Assessor Certification in Wisconsin

An assessor-certification program for Wisconsin was authorized in 1975. Its objective is to upgrade the quality of the individual assessor. The program requires training, which is available from the Wisconsin Department of Revenue; the Vocational, Technical and Adult Education districts; and other private sources. As of January 1977, all local assessors in Wisconsin must be certified by representatives of the Wisconsin Department of Revenue prior to assuming office as local assessors. *The goal of the program is to establish, by means of a testing procedure, minimum standards of knowledge for local assessors and other assessment personnel* (excluding clerical support personnel) and, thus, to *improve the equity of assessments* made at the local level. The certification program does not guarantee that assessors will be proficient in their work, but it does ensure, through written examination, that they have sufficient preparation and knowledge to perform the complex functions associated with property assessment in accordance with Wisconsin law. The new law does not affect the selection of assessors. The program merely requires that the candidates for assessment offices in the municipalities of the state obtain a certificate for the class of municipality they intend to serve, prior to assuming office.

Each municipality in Wisconsin is rated for a specific level of certification for the statutory assessor, depending on the complexity of the property-assessment function. *New assessors elected or appointed on or after January 1, 1977, must obtain the level of certification appropriate for their municipalities prior to being eligible to assume office.* If a person is elected to the office of assessor on or after January 1, 1977, and is not certified at the appropriate level for that municipality, the office is declared vacant and the proper authority must appoint an appropriately certified person to assume the office of assessor. The certification rules also apply to new property-assessment personnel, other than the statutory assessor, who are appointed on or after January 1, 1977. The level of required certification for assessment personnel is determined by their duties. Each certification level has a description of the duties authorized within that level. To legally perform any or all of the duties described at a particular level of certification, a person must be certified at that level.

Assessor Certification Examination

Certification may be attained by successfully completing the examination required by the Wisconsin Department of Revenue for that particular level of certification. All certifications issued prior to January 1, 1981, are valid for ten years from the date of issuance. All certifications issued on or after January 1, 1981, expire on the sixth June 1 following the date of issuance. Individuals may be recertified by successfully completing the current certification examination or by meeting the established continuing-education requirements and attending at least four of the five annual assessor schools held during the five years preceding their certification expiration dates.

On January 1, 1981, a temporary certification status was initiated. A temporarily certified individual is authorized to perform, in accordance with the Wisconsin Property Assessment Manual and under the direct supervision of the certified assessor, the duties defined for the lowest assessment-technician level of assessor certification. Applications for temporary certification must be in writing on the prescribed form. Approval is based on the conditions that the applicant has not been temporarily certified before and has a job commitment in the assessment field. Temporary certification becomes effective with the mailing of the approval letter. Temporary certification is valid until the results of the next assessor certification exam are issued or 100 days have expired since the temporary certification became effective, whichever occurs first. An applicant is restricted to challenging only one examination per exam cycle. A $20 examination fee is required for each examination.

The assessor certification program offers five levels of certification, three of which are for assessors and two of which are for other assessment personnel. Certification levels from lowest to highest are: Assessment Technician, Property Appraiser, Assessor 1, Assessor 2 and Assessor 3. With the exception of the Assessor 3 level, which is unique, each level of certification is progressively more demanding and encompasses the duties of the lower levels. A person certified as an Assessor 2 thus automatically is certified and eligible to perform the duties of an Assessor 1, a Property Appraiser or an Assessment Technician. The Assessor 3 level is primarily for administrative property-assessment positions, so certification at that level authorizes an individual to perform only the duties prescribed at that level.

Examinations for each of the five certification levels are independent of each other and are not progressive in nature. In other words, a person does not need to complete a certification examination at one level before taking the examination for the next higher level. The exams are offered quarterly. The February and August exams are held only in Madison. The May and November exams are offered in Eau Claire, Green Bay, Madison, Pewaukee and Wausau.

QUESTIONS

1. Real estate taxes in Wisconsin are usually

    1. paid to the assessor of each municipality.
    2. prepaid on January 31 of the tax year.
    3. prepaid on May 1 of the tax year.
    4. paid in arrears on or before January 31 of the year following the levy.

2. A property owner may redeem his or her property from delinquent taxes by paying all past-due taxes plus

    1. a penalty of 2 percent per month.
    2. a penalty of 3 percent per month.
    3. a penalty of 5 percent per month.
    4. penalties and interest within three years from the delinquency entry.

3. For Wisconsin, a construction-lien claim made by a prime contractor must be filed

    1. with the treasurer of the municipality.
    2. with the building inspector of the municipality.
    3. within two months after completing the work.
    4. within six months after completing the work and at least 30 days after the warning notice.

4. The market value of a residence is established at $53,400. If the municipality assesses at 60 percent of the market value, what is the assessed value of the property?

    1. $8,900
    2. $21,360
    3. $32,040
    4. None of the above

5. The assessed value of a home is $48,650. If the tax rate is $.0184 per $1 of assessed value, what is the amount of property tax due on the property?

    1. $264.40
    2. $447.58
    3. $895.16
    4. None of the above

6. To take an assessor certification test, an applicant must

    1. be a licensed real estate broker.
    2. pay a $20 examination fee.
    3. be 18 years of age.
    4. be an experienced appraiser.

7. An assessor elected or appointed in Wisconsin after January 1977 must

    1. be certified at the Assessor 3 level.
    2. be certified at the Assessor 1 level.
    3. be certified at the appropriate level for his or her municipality before being eligible to assume office.
    4. apply to take a certification exam after being elected.

8. The annual real estate tax in Wisconsin is levied as of what date for each calendar year?

    1. December 31   3. January 31
    2. January 1   4. February 28

9. You are filing an objection to the assessed valuation on your home. You make your objection to which of the following?

    1. The mayor's office
    2. The Register of Deeds
    3. The Wisconsin Department of Revenue
    4. The Board of Review

10. The maximum penalty for delinquent real estate in Wisconsin is how much per month?

    1. ½ percent   3. 1½ percent
    2. 1 percent   4. 2 percent

11. One of your tenants recently moved out of his apartment prior to the expiration of his lease. The court has issued a judgment against the tenant and it has been recorded. The judgment will remain a lien against the tenant for how many years?

    1. One   3. Five
    2. Three   4. Ten

10

Real Estate Contracts

The contract for the sale of real estate, known in Wisconsin as an *offer to purchase,* is the most important document in a real estate sales transaction. It fixes the rights and duties of the parties to the transaction and controls all the subsequent proceedings, including the consummation of the transaction (the closing). A sample form is included in this chapter.

BROKER'S AUTHORITY TO PREPARE DOCUMENTS

A Wisconsin licensee is prohibited from giving advice or opinions regarding the legal rights or obligations of parties to a transaction, the legal effect of contracts or conveyances, or the state of title to real estate. Any licensee or registrant who violates these rules is in violation of the Wisconsin statute that relates to investigations and the revocation of licenses.

Contract Forms

A licensee or registrant may prepare and use only forms that have been approved by the Wisconsin Department of Regulation and Licensing or by the State Bar of Wisconsin. In addition, RL16.03 identifies other approved forms such as selected Uniform Commercial Code forms and forms for the sale and rental of real estate or a business opportunity located in another state. The approved forms may be prepared and used subject to the following conditions:

1. Approved forms may be used only when a licensee is acting as an agent or a party in a real estate or business opportunity transaction. A broker must now use approved listing contracts, except as otherwise provided in RL16.04.

2. Salespeople may use any WB form prepared by the Department of Regulation and Licensing.

3. A non-approved form may be used when the department has no approved form for a given kind of real estate or business opportunity transaction.

4. A non-approved form may be used for a property management agreement between a broker and a landlord—prepared by the broker entering into the agreement, the broker's attorney or the landlord—that contains provisions relating to leasing, managing, marketing and the overall management of the landlord's property.

5. RL16.06 covers specifics relating to the use of addenda to real estate contracts.

Licensees who use outdated forms violate Section 452.14(3)(m) of the Wisconsin Statutes and RL16. Some of these forms appear on all salesperson and broker license examinations.

This material supplements Chapter 10 in *Modern Real Estate Practice* by Galaty, Allaway and Kyle.

ESSENTIALS OF A VALID CONTRACT

The six essential elements of a valid real estate contract described in Chapter 10 of the text generally are applicable to Wisconsin.

Statute of Frauds

The Wisconsin Statute of Frauds requires that all documents conveying interest in real estate, including transactions by which land is created, transferred, mortgaged, assigned or otherwise affected, are in writing and are signed by the parties. Leases for one year or less are not subject to the statute of frauds.

Competent Parties

In Wisconsin, the legal age for entering into a contract is 18. *A contract entered into with a minor is voidable at the option of the minor* because the minor can renounce, or void, the contract at any time during the minority period and for a reasonable time thereafter. After reaching legal age, the former minor can ratify, or confirm in writing and be bound by, any such contract that previously has not been voided. However, the laws are constructed to protect young persons from adults who might take advantage of them. Persons entering into a contract with a minor do so at their own risk.

Offer and Acceptance

After an offer to purchase is accepted by the seller, it becomes a binding contract on both buyer and seller. If the meaning of a contract is questioned by either the buyer or the seller, or its wording is vague, the courts usually will rule against the party who drafted it. Licensees, therefore, must be careful when drafting the offer to purchase.

Equitable Title

In Wisconsin, after a contract is accepted, *the doctrine of equitable conversion* takes effect. *Under this doctrine, the buyer becomes the owner, subject to his or her liability to pay the rest of the purchase price.* The seller has only a claim for the rest of the purchase price and holds title to the property only as security to ensure that the price is paid. In other words, the seller is still in possession, but holds the property subject to a legal obligation to take care of it for the buyer. The buyer, then, holds *equitable title* to the real estate.

TERMS OF THE CONTRACT

The offer to purchase should contain the following elements: the *nature of the estate to be conveyed, whether it is fee simple or some other estate;* the *form of the deed to be used;* the *total consideration;* the *method of payment;* an *accurate legal description* of the property; and the *date and place for the closing.* When a contract provides that *"time is of the essence,"* its terms must be carried out exactly by the date specified unless an extension is mutually agreed on by the parties.

If a *counteroffer* is made, it should be made on the department-approved counteroffer forms (WB-44 or WB-46). If a later change must be made that is mutually agreeable to the parties, Form WB-43 (Amendment to Contract of Sale) should be used.

Encumbrances and Other Conditions

Sellers should be careful to include in the sale only what they own. All restrictions, limitations or encumbrances on the property or its use should be stated fully and the contract should specify that the property is being sold subject to them. If applicable, the *offer to purchase also should state any contingencies or conditions* that must be met before the contract can be performed. For example, if the purchaser must borrow money in order to make the purchase, the details of the mortgage loan he or she expects to obtain should be included, along with a statement that the contract is to be performed subject to the purchaser's obtaining such a loan. The more details included in describing contingencies, the less confusion there will be as to whether they have been met. Provision also should be made for the division of any rents, insurance premiums, taxes, water charges or interest on existing mortgages. Title insurance cannot be assumed or transferred in Wisconsin.

Personal Property

Any personal property to be included in the sale, such as air-conditioning units, carpets, drapes, refrigerators or ranges, *also should be specified in the sales contract.* This will minimize the possibility of a conflict between the buyer and seller regarding what constitutes fixtures and what constitutes personal property. The broker or salesperson should bring to both parties' attention any property that might be in question. The disposition of annual crops in the sale of farmland is included in this classification and must be specified in the offer to purchase.

Signatures

The *offer to purchase must be signed by the parties*. When selling property owned by a married person, it is important to obtain the *signatures of both spouses* in order to release any *homestead rights* the owner's spouse may have in the property. When financing is necessary for the buyers, the lender will want both spouses to sign the accepted offer to show the willingness of both spouses to sign the mortgage and the note.

The Marital Property Act raises the question of what role real estate licensees play in clarifying with married sellers how their property was owned or controlled by one or the other or both of them and with married buyers how they will want to own and take title to the property. Under the new law, title does not determine who has ownership rights to property. However, title generally does determine management and control rights of the property. In much the same way that title determined management rights under the common-law property system, the marital property law generally looks at who "holds" the property (holding property usually means having title to property) and at the classification of the property. "Management and control" are broadly defined under the law as "the right to buy, sell, use, transfer, exchange, abandon, lease, consume, expend, assign, create a security interest in, mortgage, encumber, dispose of, institute or defend a civil action regarding or otherwise deal with property as if it were property of an unmarried person."

The law provides that a spouse *acting alone* may manage and control

1. the spouse's individual property;

2. unless otherwise provided, marital property held in the spouse's name alone or not held in the name of either spouse;

3. marital property held in the names of both spouses in the alternative (e.g., "John *or* Mary");

4. subject to exceptions, all marital property for the purpose of obtaining an extension of certain kinds of credit for an obligation in the interest of the marriage or family;

5. a policy of insurance, if the spouse is designated as the owner on the records of the issuer of the policy;

6. any right of an employee under a deferred employment benefit plan (e.g., pension plan) that accrues as a result of the spouse's employment; or

7. any legal claim for relief of the spouse.

Only by *acting together* may spouses manage and control marital property held in the names of both spouses (e.g., "John *and* Mary") unless the property is held in the alternative.

The right to manage and control marital property transferred to a trust is determined by the terms of the trust.

The classifications of property are more complex than before the Marital Property Act went into effect, and licensees will have to avoid giving legal advice, especially concerning how buyers will hold property.

The board has taken the position in the past that interspousal disputes concerning the disposition of their property may require disclosure to buyers who could be inconvenienced and adversely affected by the situation. This position is not changed by the Marital Property Act.

AN EXPLANATION OF THE OFFER TO PURCHASE

Information contained in this chapter is provided to assist applicants as well as licensees to understand the new WB-11 residential offer to purchase. This chapter includes both a sample and a line-by-line explanation of the offer to purchase.

HIGHLIGHTS OF CHANGES REFLECTED IN THE NEW WB-11 RESIDENTIAL OFFER TO PURCHASE

1. The new offer is four pages long and contains optional contingency provisions.

2. A complete legal description is no longer necessarily required in all offers.

3. The list of fixtures has been expanded.

4. Prorations are to be made through the day prior to closing.

5. The buyer is given the right to inspect the property within three days before closing.

6. The broker's role as the holder of earnest money has been clarified.

7. Optional contingencies are included in the offer and may be made part of the contract.

Sample Offer To Purchase

On November 15, 1994, salesperson James obtained an offer from Jay and Linda Jones to purchase the Carter property for $56,000. The offer was made on the basis of the buyers' assumption of the balance of the existing mortgage and the balance of the selling price being paid in cash at closing. Possession was desired as of the date of closing, which was to be no later than December 15, 1994. If the Carters occupy the property after the closing, they agree to pay $25 per day for each day they

Figure 10.1   Residential Offer To Purchase

Approved by Wisconsin Department of Regulation and Licensing
11-1-93 (Optional Use Date)
2-1-94 (Mandatory Use Date)

Wisconsin Legal Blank Co., Inc.
Milwaukee, Wisconsin

WB-11 RESIDENTIAL OFFER TO PURCHASE

1   THE BROKER DRAFTING THIS OFFER ON __November 15, 1994__ (DATE) IS THE AGENT OF (SELLER)(BUYER) [STRIKE AS APPLICABLE]

2   **GENERAL PROVISIONS**   The Buyer, __Jay Jones and Linda Jones, Husband and Wife__,
3   offers to purchase the Property known as [Street Address] __1400 Regas Lane__
4   in the __city__ of __Madison__, County of __Dane__, Wisconsin.
5   *(Additional description, if any:)* __Lot 2, Block 4, Fairmount Subdivision NW¼ of Section B, T9N, R7E,__
6   __Dane County, Wisconsin__ on the following terms:
7   ■ PURCHASE PRICE: __Fifty-Six Thousand and 00/100__
8   _____ Dollars ($ __56,000__).
9   ■ EARNEST MONEY of $ __2,000__ in the form of __Check__ accompanies this Offer and earnest
10 money of $ __2,000__ in the form of __Check__ will be paid within __upon__ days of acceptance.
11 ■ THE BALANCE OF THE PURCHASE PRICE will be paid in cash or equivalent at closing unless otherwise provided below.
12 ■ ADDITIONAL ITEMS INCLUDED IN PURCHASE PRICE: Seller shall include in the purchase price and transfer, free and clear of
13 encumbrances, all fixtures, as defined at lines 194 to 202 and as may be on the Property on the date of this Offer, unless excluded at lines
14 16-17, and the following additional items: __All carpeting, drapes and drapery rods, refrigerator, washer__
15 __and dryer__
16 ■ ITEMS NOT INCLUDED IN THE PURCHASE PRICE: _____
17 _____
18 ■ PROPERTY CONDITION REPRESENTATIONS: Seller represents to Buyer that as of the date of acceptance Seller has no notice or
19 knowledge of conditions affecting the Property or transaction (as defined at lines 168 to 188) other than those identified in Seller's Real
20 Estate Condition Report dated _____ which was received by Buyer prior to Buyer signing this Offer
21 [COMPLETE DATE OR STRIKE AS APPLICABLE] and __None__
22 _____
23 ■ TIME IS OF THE ESSENCE as to: (1) Earnest money payment(s); (2) binding acceptance; (3) occupancy; (4) date of closing
24 [STRIKE AS APPLICABLE] and all other dates and deadlines in this Offer except: _____.

25 **OPTIONAL PROVISIONS AND ADDENDA**   See lines 225 to 270 for optional provisions including contingencies. See line 271 to determine if
26 addenda, riders or other documents have been made a part of this Offer.

27 **ADDITIONAL PROVISIONS**   __Buyers wish to assume sellers' existing mortgage with approximate__
28 __balance of $26,500 and seller's home insurance policy which runs until April 30, 1995__
29 _____

30 **ACCEPTANCE, DELIVERY AND RELATED PROVISIONS**

31 ■ BINDING ACCEPTANCE: This Offer is binding upon both parties only if a copy of the accepted Offer is delivered to Buyer on or
32 before __November 17, 1994__. *CAUTION: This Offer may be withdrawn prior to delivery of the accepted Offer.*
33 ■ DELIVERY OF DOCUMENTS AND WRITTEN NOTICES: Unless otherwise stated in this Offer, delivery of documents and written
34 notices to a party shall be effective only when accomplished in any of the following ways:
35 (1) By depositing the document or written notice postage or fees prepaid in the U.S. Mail or a commercial delivery system addressed to the
36 party at: Buyer: _____
37 Seller: _____
38 (2) By giving the document or written notice personally to the party;
39 (3) By electronically transmitting the document or written notice to the following telephone number:
40 Buyer: _____ (_____) _____   Seller: _____ (_____) _____

41 **OCCUPANCY AND RELATED PROVISIONS**

42 ■ OCCUPANCY of _____ shall be given to Buyer
43 at time of closing unless otherwise provided in this Offer (lines 252 through 255). At time of Buyer's occupancy, Property shall be free of all
44 debris and personal property except for personal property belonging to current tenants, or that sold to Buyer or left with Buyer's consent.
45 ■ LEASED PROPERTY: If Property is currently leased and leases extend beyond closing, Seller shall assign Seller's rights under said
46 lease(s) and transfer all security deposits and prepaid rents thereunder to Buyer at closing. The terms of the (written)(oral) [STRIKE ONE]
47 lease(s), if any, are _____
48 ■ RENTAL WEATHERIZATION: This transaction (is)(is not) [STRIKE ONE] exempt from State of Wisconsin Rental Weatherization Standards
49 (ILHR 67, Wisconsin Administrative Code). If not exempt, (Buyer)(Seller) [STRIKE ONE] will be responsible for compliance, including all costs.

50 **CLOSING AND RELATED PROVISIONS**

51 ■ CLOSING: This transaction is to be closed at the place designated by Buyer's mortgagee or __New House Realty__
52 _____ no later than __December 15__, 19__94__ unless another date or place is agreed to in writing.
53 ■ CLOSING PRORATIONS: The following items shall be prorated at closing: real estate taxes, rents, water and sewer use charges,
54 garbage pick-up and other private and municipal charges, property owner's association assessments, fuel and _____
55 _____. Any income, taxes or expenses shall accrue to Seller, and be prorated, through the day prior to closing.
56 Net general real estate taxes shall be prorated based on (the net general real estate taxes for the current year, if known, otherwise on the
57 net general real estate taxes for the preceeding year)(_____
58 _____). [STRIKE AND COMPLETE AS APPLICABLE] *CAUTION: If Property has not been fully assessed for*
59 *tax purposes (for example, new construction, remodeling or completed/pending reassessment) or if proration on the basis of net general*
60 *real estate taxes is not acceptable (for example, changing mill rate, lottery credits), insert estimated annual tax or other basis for proration.*
61 ■ SPECIAL ASSESSMENTS: Special assessments, if any, for work on site actually commenced or levied prior to date of this Offer shall be
62 paid by Seller no later than closing. All other special assessments shall be paid by Buyer. *CAUTION: Consider a special agreement if area*
63 *assessments or property owner's association assessments are contemplated.*
64 ■ FORM OF TITLE EVIDENCE: Seller shall give evidence of title by Seller's choice of: (1) an abstract of title; or (2) an owner's policy of
65 title insurance [STRIKE AS APPLICABLE] as further described at lines 147 to 161.
66 ■ CONVEYANCE OF TITLE: Upon payment of the purchase price, Seller shall convey the Property by warranty deed (or other
67 conveyance as provided herein) free and clear of all liens and encumbrances, except: municipal and zoning ordinances and agreements
68 entered under them, recorded easements for the distribution of utility and municipal services, recorded building and use restrictions and
69 covenants, general taxes levied in the year of closing and _____
70 (provided none of the foregoing prohibit present use of the Property), which constitutes merchantable title for purposes of this transaction.
71 Seller further agrees to complete and execute the documents necessary to record the conveyance. *WARNING: Municipal and zoning*

Figure 10.1 Residential Offer To Purchase (continued)

72 *ordinances, recorded building and use restrictions, covenants and easements may prohibit certain improvements or uses and therefore*
73 *should be reviewed, particularly if Buyer contemplates making improvements to Property or a use other than the current use.*

74 **PROPERTY CONDITION PROVISIONS**

75 ■ REAL ESTATE CONDITION REPORT: Wisconsin law requires sellers of property which includes 1-4 dwelling units to provide buyers
76 with a Real Estate Condition Report. Excluded from this requirement are sales of property that has never been inhabited, sales exempt from
77 the real estate transfer fee, and sales by certain fiduciaries, (for example, personal representatives who have never occupied the Property).
78 The form of the Report is found in Wis. Stats. §709.03. The law provides: "709.02 Disclosure . . . the owner of the property shall furnish, not
79 later than 10 days after acceptance of the contract of sale, to the prospective buyer of the property a completed copy of the report . . . A
80 prospective buyer who does not receive a report within the ten days, may within two business days after the end of that ten day period,
81 rescind the contract of sale by delivering a written notice of rescission to the seller or the seller's agent." Buyer may also have certain
82 rescission rights if a Real Estate Condition Report disclosing defects is furnished before expiration of the 10 days, but after the Offer is
83 submitted to Seller. Buyer should review the report form or consult with an attorney for additional information regarding these rescission
84 rights.
85 ■ PROPERTY MEASUREMENT AND TOTAL SQUARE FOOTAGE: Buyer acknowledges that there are various formulas used to
86 calculate total square footage and that total square footage figures will vary dependent upon the formula used. Buyer also acknowledges
87 that all room and house measurements may be approximate because of rounding or other reasons. *CAUTION: Buyer should verify total*
88 *square footage formula and room measurements if material to Buyer's decision to purchase.*
89 ■ INSPECTIONS: Seller agrees to allow Buyer's inspectors reasonable access to the Property, upon reasonable notice. Buyer agrees to
90 promptly provide copies of all inspection reports to Seller, and to listing broker if Property is listed.
91 ■ PROPERTY DAMAGE BETWEEN ACCEPTANCE AND CLOSING: Seller shall maintain the Property until the earlier of closing or
92 occupancy of Buyer in materially the same condition as of the date of acceptance of this Offer, except for ordinary wear and tear. If, prior to
93 the earlier of closing or occupancy of Buyer, the Property is damaged in an amount of not more than five percent (5%) of the selling price,
94 Seller shall be obligated to repair the Property and restore it to the same condition that it was on the day of this Offer. If the damage shall
95 exceed such sum, Seller shall promptly notify Buyer in writing of the damage and this Offer may be cancelled at option of Buyer. Should
96 Buyer elect to carry out this Offer despite such damage, Buyer shall be entitled to the insurance proceeds relating to the damage to the
97 Property, plus a credit towards the purchase price equal to the amount of Seller's deductible on such policy. However, if this sale is financed
98 by a land contract or a mortgage to Seller, the insurance proceeds shall be held in trust for the sole purpose of restoring the Property.
99 ■ PRE-CLOSING INSPECTION: At a reasonable time, preapproved by Seller or Seller's agent, within 3 days before closing, Buyer shall
100 have the right to inspect the Property to determine that there has been no significant change in the condition of the Property, except for
101 ordinary wear and tear and changes approved by Buyer, and that any defects Seller has elected to cure have been repaired in a good and
102 workmanlike manner.

103 **DEFAULT**

104 Seller and Buyer each have the legal duty to use good faith and due diligence in completing the terms and conditions of this Offer. A
105 material failure to perform any obligation under this Offer is a default which may subject the defaulting party to liability for damages or other
106 legal remedies.
107 If Buyer defaults, Seller may:
108 (1) sue for specific performance and request the earnest money as partial payment of the purchase price; or
109 (2) terminate the Offer and have the option to: (a) request the earnest money as liquidated damages; or (b) direct Broker to return the
110 earnest money and have the option to sue for actual damages.
111 If Seller defaults, Buyer may:
112 (1) sue for specific performance; or
113 (2) terminate the Offer and request the return of the earnest money, sue for actual damages, or both.
114 In addition, the Parties may seek any other remedies available in law or equity.
115 The Parties understand that the availability of any judicial remedy will depend upon the circumstances of the situation and the discretion
116 of the courts. If either Party defaults, the Parties may renegotiate the Offer or seek nonjudicial dispute resolution instead of the remedies
117 outlined above. By agreeing to binding arbitration, the Parties may lose the right to litigate in a court of law those disputes covered by the
118 arbitration agreement.

119 **NOTE:** WISCONSIN LICENSE LAW PROHIBITS A BROKER FROM GIVING ADVICE OR OPINIONS CONCERNING THE LEGAL
120 RIGHTS OR OBLIGATIONS OF PARTIES TO A TRANSACTION OR THE LEGAL EFFECT OF A SPECIFIC CONTRACT OR
121 CONVEYANCE. AN ATTORNEY SHOULD BE CONSULTED IF LEGAL ADVICE IS REQUIRED. Buyer's or Seller's legal right to
122 earnest money cannot be determined by Broker. In the absence of a mutual agreement by the Parties, earnest money will be
123 distributed as set forth in lines 125 to 146.

124 **EARNEST MONEY**

125 ■ HELD BY: Earnest money, if held by a broker, shall be held in the trust account of the broker drafting the Offer prior to acceptance of
126 Offer and in the trust account of the listing broker (buyer's agent if Property is not listed) after acceptance until applied to purchase price or
127 otherwise disbursed as provided in the Offer. If negotiations do not result in an accepted offer, the earnest money shall be promptly
128 disbursed (after clearance from payor's depository institution if earnest money is paid by check) to the person who paid the earnest
129 money. *CAUTION: If someone other than Buyer makes payment of earnest money on behalf of Buyer, consider a special agreement*
130 *regarding disbursement.*
131 ■ DISBURSEMENT: At closing, earnest money shall be disbursed according to the closing statement. If this Offer does not close, the
132 earnest money shall be disbursed according to a written disbursement agreement signed by all Parties to this Offer. If said disbursement
133 agreement has not been delivered to broker within 60 days after the date set for closing, broker may disburse the earnest money: (1) as
134 directed by an attorney who has reviewed the transaction and does not represent Buyer or Seller; (2) into a court hearing a lawsuit involving
135 the earnest money and all Parties to this Offer; (3) as directed by court order; or (4) any other disbursement required or allowed by law.
136 Broker may retain legal services to direct disbursement per (1) or to file an interpleader action per (2) and broker may deduct from the
137 earnest money any costs and reasonable attorneys fees, not to exceed $250, prior to disbursement. Should persons other than broker hold
138 earnest money, an escrow agreement should be drafted by the Parties or an attorney for Buyer or Seller.
139 ■ LEGAL RIGHTS/ACTION: Broker's disbursement of earnest money does not determine the legal rights of the Parties in relation to this
140 Offer. At least 30 days prior to disbursement per (1) or (4), broker shall send Buyer and Seller notice of the disbursement by certified mail. If
141 Buyer or Seller disagree with broker's proposed disbursement, a lawsuit may be filed to obtain a court order regarding disbursement. Small
142 Claims Court has jurisdiction over all earnest money disputes arising out of the sale of residential property with 1-4 dwelling units and
143 certain other earnest money disputes. The Buyer and Seller should consider consulting attorneys regarding their legal rights under this
144 Offer in case of a dispute.
145 Both parties agree to hold the broker harmless from any liability for good faith disbursement of earnest money in accordance with this
146 Offer or applicable Department of Regulation and Licensing regulations concerning earnest money. See Wis. Administrative Code RL 18.

Figure 10.1 Residential Offer To Purchase (continued)

147 **TITLE EVIDENCE**

148 ■ FORM OF TITLE EVIDENCE: Seller shall give evidence of title (as selected at lines 64 to 65) to the Property in the form of: (1) an
149 abstract of title prepared by an attorney licensed to practice law in Wisconsin or an abstract company; or (2) an owner's policy of title
150 insurance in the amount of the purchase price on a current ALTA form issued by an insurer licensed to write title insurance in Wisconsin.
151 ■ PROVISION OF MERCHANTABLE TITLE: Seller shall pay all costs of providing such title evidence. For purposes of closing, title
152 evidence shall be acceptable if the abstract or a commitment for the required title insurance is delivered to Buyer's attorney or to Buyer not
153 less than 3 business days before closing, showing title to the Property as of a date no more than 15 days before delivery of such title
154 evidence to be merchantable, subject only to liens which will be paid out of the proceeds of closing and standard abstract certificate
155 limitations or standard title insurance requirements and exceptions, as appropriate.
156 ■ TITLE ACCEPTABLE FOR CLOSING: If title is not acceptable for closing, Buyer shall notify Seller in writing of objections to title by
157 the time set for closing. In such event, Seller shall have a reasonable time, but not exceeding 15 days, to remove the objections, and the time
158 for closing shall be extended as necessary for this purpose. In the event that Seller is unable to remove said objections, Buyer shall have 5
159 days from receipt of notice thereof, to deliver written notice waiving the objections, and the time for closing shall be extended accordingly.
160 If Buyer does not waive objections, this Offer shall be null and void. Providing title evidence acceptable for closing does not extinguish
161 Seller's obligations to give merchantable title to Buyer.

162 **ENTIRE CONTRACT**

163 This Offer, including any amendments to it, contains the entire agreement of the Buyer and Seller regarding the transaction. All prior
164 negotiations and discussions have been merged into this Offer. This agreement binds and inures to the benefit of the Parties to this Offer
165 and their successors in interest.

DEFINITIONS

167 ■ ACCEPTANCE: Acceptance occurs when all Buyers and Sellers have signed the Offer. See lines 31 and 32 regarding binding acceptance.
168 ■ CONDITIONS AFFECTING THE PROPERTY OR TRANSACTION: A "condition affecting the Property or transaction" is defined as follows:
169 (a) planned or commenced public improvements which may result in special assessments or otherwise materially affect the Property or
170 the present use of the Property;
171 (b) government agency or court order requiring repair, alteration or correction of any existing condition;
172 (c) structural inadequacies which if not repaired will significantly shorten the expected normal life of the Property;
173 (d) mechanical systems inadequate for the present use of the Property;
174 (e) conditions constituting a significant health or safety hazard for occupants of Property;
175 (f) insect or animal infestation of the Property;
176 (g) underground storage tanks on the Property for storage of flammable or combustible liquids including but not limited to gasoline and
177 heating oil; *NOTE: Wis. Adm. Code, Chapter ILHR 10 contains registration and operation rules for such underground storage tanks.*
178 (h) any portion of the Property being in a 100 year floodplain, a wetland or a shoreland zoning area under local, state or federal regulations;
179 (i) completed or pending reassessment of the Property for property tax purposes;
180 (j) material violations of environmental rules or other rules or agreements regulating the use of the Property;
181 (k) construction or remodeling on Property for which required state or local permits had not been obtained;
182 (l) any land division involving the subject Property, for which required state or local approvals had not been obtained;
183 (m) material violation of applicable state or local smoke detector laws; *NOTE: State law requires smoke detectors on all levels of all*
184 *residential properties.*
185 (n) high voltage electric (100 KV or greater) or steel natural gas transmission lines located on but not directly serving the Property;
186 (o) that a structure on the Property is designated as a historic building or that any part of the Property is in a historic district;
187 (p) other conditions or occurrences which would significantly reduce the value of the Property to a reasonable person with knowledge of
188 the nature and scope of the condition or occurrence. See lines 18 to 22.
189 ■ DAYS: Deadlines expressed as a specific number of "days" from the occurrence of an event, such as acceptance, are calculated by
190 excluding the day the event occurred. The deadline then expires at midnight on the last day. Deadlines expressed as a specific number of
191 "business days" exclude Saturdays, Sundays and any legal public holiday under Wisconsin or Federal law, or other holiday designated by
192 the President such that the postal service does not receive registered mail or make regular deliveries on that day. Deadlines expressed as a
193 specific day of the calendar year or as the day of a specific event, such as closing, expire at midnight of that day.
194 ■ FIXTURES: A "fixture" is an item of property which is physically attached to or so closely associated with land or buildings so as to be
195 treated as part of the real estate, including, without limitation, physically attached items not easily removable without damage to the
196 premises, items specifically adapted to the premises, and items customarily treated as fixtures including but not limited to all: garden bulbs;
197 plants; shrubs and trees; screen and storm doors and windows; electric lighting fixtures; window shades; curtain and traverse rods; blinds
198 and shutters; central heating and cooling units and attached equipment; water heaters and softeners; sump pumps; attached or fitted floor
199 coverings; awnings; attached antennas, satellite dishes and component parts; garage door openers and remote controls; installed security
200 systems; central vacuum systems and accessories; in-ground sprinkler systems and component parts; built-in appliances; ceiling fans;
201 fences; storage buildings on permanent foundations and docks/piers on permanent foundations. See lines 12 to 17. *CAUTION: Address*
202 *rented fixtures, if any, e.g. water softener, L.P. tanks, etc.*
203 ■ TIME IS OF THE ESSENCE: If "Time is of the Essence" applies to a date or deadline, failure to perform by the exact date or deadline is a
204 breach of contract. If "Time is of the Essence" does not apply to a date or deadline, then performance within a reasonable time of the date or
205 deadline is allowed before a breach occurs. See lines 23 and 24.

206 **PROVISIONS RELATED TO FINANCING**

207 ■ LOAN COMMITMENT: If this Offer is contingent on financing, Buyer agrees to pay all customary financing costs (including closing
208 fees), to apply for financing promptly, and to provide evidence of application promptly upon request of Seller. If Buyer qualifies for said
209 financing or other financing acceptable to Buyer, Buyer agrees to deliver to Seller, or Seller's agent, a copy of the written loan commitment
210 no later than the deadline for loan commitment under the Financing Contingency. If Buyer does not make timely delivery of said
211 commitment, Seller may terminate this Offer if Seller delivers a written notice of termination to Buyer prior to Seller's actual receipt of a
212 copy of Buyer's written loan commitment.
213 ■ FINANCING UNAVAILABILITY: If this Offer is contingent on financing and financing is not available on the terms stated, Buyer shall
214 promptly deliver written notice to Seller of same including copies of lender(s)' rejection letter(s) or other evidence of unavailability. Unless a
215 specific loan source is named in the financing contingency, Seller shall then have 5 days to give Buyer written notice of Seller's decision to
216 finance this transaction on the same terms set forth herein, and this Offer shall remain in full force and effect, with the time for closing
217 extended accordingly. If Seller's notice is not timely given, this Offer shall be null and void.
218 ■ LAND CONTRACT: If this Offer provides for a land contract, prior to execution of the land contract Seller shall provide the same
219 evidence of merchantable title as required above and written proof, at or before execution, that the total underlying indebtedness, if any, is not
220 in excess of the proposed balance of the land contract, that the payments on the land contract are sufficient to meet all of the obligations of
221 Seller on the underlying indebtedness, and that all creditors whose consent is required have consented to the land contract sale.

Figure 10.1 Residential Offer To Purchase (continued)

222 **PROPERTY ADDRESS:** 1400 Regas Lane _____ page 4 of 4

223 **OPTIONAL PROVISIONS: THE PROVISIONS ON LINES 225 THROUGH 271 ARE A PART OF THIS OFFER IF MARKED,**
224 **SUCH AS WITH AN "X". THEY ARE NOT PART OF THIS OFFER IF MARKED N/A OR ARE LEFT BLANK.**

225 ☐ **FINANCING CONTINGENCY:** *This Offer is contingent upon Buyer being able to obtain, within _____ days of acceptance*
226 *of this Offer, a _____* [INSERT LOAN PROGRAM] *(fixed)(adjustable)* [STRIKE ONE] *rate first mortgage loan*
227 *commitment, in an amount of not less than $_____ for a term of not less than _____ years, amortized over not less*
228 *than _____ years. If the purchase price under this Offer is modified, the loan amount, unless otherwise provided, shall be adjusted to*
229 *the same percentage of the purchase price as in this contingency and the monthly payments shall be adjusted as necessary to maintain the*
230 *term and amortization stated above.*
231 *IF FINANCING IS FIXED RATE the annual rate of interest shall not exceed _____% and monthly payments of principal and*
232 *interest shall not exceed $_____.*
233 *IF FINANCING IS ADJUSTABLE RATE the initial annual interest rate shall not exceed _____%. The initial interest rate shall be*
234 *fixed for _____ months, at which time the interest rate may be increased not more than _____% per year. The maximum*
235 *interest rate during the mortgage term shall not exceed _____%. Initial monthly payments of principal and interest shall not exceed*
236 *$_____. Monthly payments of principal and interest may be adjusted to reflect interest changes.*
237 *MONTHLY PAYMENTS MAY ALSO INCLUDE 1/12th of the estimated net annual real estate taxes, hazard insurance premiums, and*
238 *private mortgage insurance premiums. The mortgage may not include a prepayment premium. Buyer agrees to pay a loan fee in an amount*
239 *not to exceed _____% of the loan. [Loan fee refers to discount points and/or loan origination fee, but DOES NOT include Buyer's*
240 *other closing costs.] SEE LINES 207 TO 221 FOR ADDITIONAL FINANCING PROVISIONS.*

241 ☐ **SALE OF BUYER'S PROPERTY CONTINGENCY:** *This Offer is contingent upon the sale and closing of Buyer's property*
242 *located at _____ , no later than _____. Seller may keep Seller's*
243 *Property on the market for sale and accept secondary offers. If Seller accepts a bona fide secondary offer, Seller may give written notice to*
244 *the Buyer of acceptance. If Buyer does not deliver a written waiver of this contingency and _____*
245 _____ [INSERT OTHER REQUIREMENTS , IF ANY, FOR EXAMPLE
246 WAIVER OF ADDITIONAL CONTINGENCIES] *within _____ hours of Buyer's actual receipt of said notice, this Offer shall be null and void.*

247 ☐ **SECONDARY OFFER:** *This Offer is secondary to a prior accepted offer. This Offer shall become primary upon delivery of written*
248 *notice to Buyer that this Offer is primary. Seller agrees to deliver said notice to Buyer promptly upon Seller's receipt of evidence satisfactory*
249 *to Seller that the prior offer is null and void. Buyer may declare this Offer null and void by delivering written notice of withdrawal to Seller*
250 *prior to delivery of Seller's notice that this Offer is primary. Buyer may give notice of withdrawal no earlier than _____ hours from*
251 *acceptance of this Offer. Offer deadlines measured from acceptance shall be measured from the time this Offer becomes primary.*

252 ☐ **OCCUPANCY AFTER CLOSING:** *Occupancy of _____*
253 *shall be given to Buyer on _____ at _____ a.m./p.m. At closing, Seller shall prepay an occupancy charge of $_____ per day*
254 *or partial day of post-closing occupancy, the unearned portion (shall)(shall not)* [STRIKE ONE] *be refundable based on actual occupancy.*
255 **CAUTION: Consider a special agreement regarding occupancy escrow, insurance, utilities, maintenance, keys, etc. If appropriate.**

256 ☐ **INSPECTION CONTINGENCY:** *This Offer is contingent upon a qualified independent inspector conducting an inspection of*
257 *the Property/or _____ which discloses*
258 *no defects as defined below. This contingency shall be deemed satisfied unless Buyer, within _____ days of acceptance, delivers to*
259 *Seller a copy of the inspector's written inspection report and a written notice listing the defects identified in the inspection report to which*
260 *Buyer objects. Buyer agrees to deliver a copy of the report and notice to Listing Broker, if Property is listed, upon delivery to Seller.*
261 ■ *RIGHT TO CURE: Seller (shall)(shall not)* [STRIKE ONE] *have a right to cure the defects. If Seller has right to cure, Seller may satisfy*
262 *this contingency by: (1) delivering a written notice of Seller's election to cure defects within 10 days of receipt of Buyer's notice; and (2)*
263 *curing the defects in a good and workmanlike manner and delivering to Buyer a written report detailing the work done no later than 3 days*
264 *prior to closing. This Offer shall be null and void if Buyer makes timely delivery of the above notice and report and: (1) Seller has a right to*
265 *cure but does not timely deliver the notice of election to cure; or (2) Seller does not have a right to cure.*
266 ■ *"DEFECT" DEFINED: For the purposes of this contingency, a defect is defined as a structural, mechanical or other condition that would*
267 *have a significant adverse effect on the value of the Property; that would significantly impair the health or safety of future occupants of the*
268 *Property; or that if not repaired, removed or replaced would significantly shorten or have a significant adverse effect on the expected*
269 *normal life of the Property. Defects do not include structural, mechanical or other conditions the nature and extent of which Buyer had*
270 *actual knowledge or written notice before signing this Offer.*
271 ☐ **OTHER:** *The attached _____ is/are made part of this Offer.*

272 **IF ACCEPTED, THIS OFFER CAN CREATE A LEGALLY ENFORCEABLE CONTRACT. BOTH PARTIES SHOULD READ THIS**
273 **DOCUMENT CAREFULLY. BROKERS MAY PROVIDE A GENERAL EXPLANATION OF THE PROVISIONS OF THE OFFER BUT ARE**
274 **PROHIBITED BY LAW FROM GIVING ADVICE OR OPINIONS CONCERNING YOUR LEGAL RIGHTS UNDER THIS OFFER OR HOW**
275 **TITLE SHOULD BE TAKEN AT CLOSING. AN ATTORNEY SHOULD BE CONSULTED IF LEGAL ADVICE IS NEEDED.**

276 This Offer was drafted on Nov. 15, 1994 [date] by [Licensee and firm] John James, New House Realty .

277 (X) _____ 426-085-1931 Nov. 15, 1994
278 (Buyer's Signature) ▲ Print Name here: ► Jay Jones (Social Security No.) (Date)

279 (X) _____ 417-214-0462 Nov. 15, 1994
280 (Buyer's Signature) ▲ Print Name here: ► Linda Jones (Social Security No.) (Date)
281 **EARNEST MONEY RECEIPT** Broker acknowledges receipt of earnest money as per line 9 of the above Offer.

282 New House Realty _____ Broker (By) John James _____

283 **SELLER ACCEPTS THIS OFFER. THE WARRANTIES, REPRESENTATIONS AND COVENANTS MADE IN THIS OFFER SURVIVE CLOSING**
284 **AND THE CONVEYANCE OF THE PROPERTY. THE UNDERSIGNED HEREBY AGREES TO CONVEY THE ABOVE-MENTIONED PROPERTY**
285 **ON THE TERMS AND CONDITIONS AS SET FORTH HEREIN AND ACKNOWLEDGES RECEIPT OF A COPY OF THIS OFFER.**

286 (x) _____ 349-382-4756 Nov. 15, 1994
287 (Seller's Signature) ▲ Print Name here: ► George Carter (Social Security No.) (Date)

288 (x) _____ 326-712-9316 Nov. 15, 1994
289 (Seller's Signature) ▲ Print Name here: ► Martha Carter (Social Security No.) (Date)

290 This Offer was presented to Seller by John James on Nov. 16 , 19 94 , at _____ a.m./p.m.

291 THIS OFFER IS REJECTED _____ _____ THIS OFFER IS COUNTERED [See attached counter] _____ _____
292 (Seller's Initials) (Date) (Seller's Initials) (Date)

remain on the property. The Joneses paid earnest money of $2,000 with another $2,000 to be paid on acceptance of the offer. The offer was accepted by the Carters on November 15, 1994.

AN OVERVIEW OF THE NEW WB-11 RESIDENTIAL OFFER TO PURCHASE

The new WB–11 residential offer to purchase is four pages long and includes optional contingency provisions, which are presented on page four of the contract.

Lines 7–11 cover the price and terms of the offer. Section 706.02(1)(c) of the Wisconsin Statutes requires that the written contract identify any material term or condition in the transaction. Foremost among these terms is the price.

Lines 12–17 are almost identical to lines 10–17 of the listing contract and were discussed under the listing contract.

Lines 18–22 are similar to lines 50–53 of the listing contract and were discussed under the listing contract.

Lines 23–24 state that "time is of the essence" for all dates and deadlines unless indicated otherwise on line 24. Lines 203–205 state that if "time is of the essence" does not apply to a date or deadline, then performance within a reasonable time of the date or deadline is allowed before a breach occurs.

Lines 25–26 indicate that optional provisions including contingencies, addenda and riders that are referenced are part of the offer.

Lines 27–29 provide for additional provisions; the previously approved offer referred to this section as special provisions.

Lines 30–40 cover acceptance, delivery and related provisions. For example, lines 31–32 state that the offer is binding on both parties only if a copy of this accepted offer is delivered to the buyer on or before the date specified on line 32.

Lines 33–40 identify the appropriate methods of delivered documents and written notice, which include mailing, personal delivery and electronic transmission (FAX).

Lines 41–49 include provision for occupancy and related provisions, including leased property and rental weatherization. It is important to note that lines 42–43 state the occupancy shall be given to the buyer at the time of <u>closing</u>. Lines 43–44 also state that the seller will take from the premises all personal property and debris except for personal property that belongs to the current tenants, or that left with the buyer's consent or sold to the buyer. Lines 45–47 state that if the property is rented, the seller must assign his or her rights under the lease(s) including security rents and prepared deposits to the buyer at closing. Lines 48–49 refer to DILHR's rental weatherization program, which is discussed in Chapter 11 of this book. The buyer and seller must determine who is to be responsible for the weatherization requirements. Note that residential property of one to four units will be occupied by the buyer for at least one year after transfer is exempt from the DILHR program as stated in Chapter 11 of this book.

Lines 50–73 cover closing and related provisions, including closing prorations, special assessments, form of title, evidence and conveyance of title. Lines 51–52 indicate that the sample transaction is to be closed at the office of the broker on or before December 15, 1994.

Lines 53–60 deal with closing prorations.

Lines 53–55 identify a substantial change in the new residential offer to purchase; <u>prorations are to be made through the day prior to closing</u>.

Lines 56–60 recognize that the tax proration may be affected by factors such as the lack of full assessment, a reassessment, a change in the mill rate or a lottery credit. Lines 64–65 state that the seller must furnish evidence of seller's choice of either an abstract of title or an owner's policy of title insurance.

Lines 66–73 cover additional exceptions to the warranty of title, such as easements, options, mortgages if assumed and long-term leases. Note that the line 68 refers to recorded easements for the distribution of utility and municipal services, which are considered to be positive easements; negative easements identified on line 185 are excluded from this section.

Lines 71–73 caution a buyer considering an improvement or change in the use of the property to review the various restrictions on the title.

Lines 74–102 deal with property condition provisions. Lines 75–84 refer to the Real Estate Condition Report that is discussed in Chapter 4 of this book.

Lines 85–88 relate to property measurement and total square footage. This section states that there are various formulas used to calculate square footage and cautions the buyer to verify total square footage and room measurements if they are material to the buyer.

Lines 89–90 state that the seller agrees to allow the buyer's inspectors access to the property and that the buyer agrees to provide copies of all inspection reports to the seller and listing broker.

Lines 91–98 deal with the handling of property in case of damage occurring prior to the earlier of closing or occupancy of buyer.

Lines 99–102 cover the pre-closing inspection; the buyer is given the right to inspect the property within three days before closing.

Lines 103–123 deal with parties' rights in the event of default. Lines 120–123 emphasize that licensees cannot give legal advice to the parties.

Lines 124–146 refer to provisions covering who will hold the earnest money, how it will be disbursed and the legal rights of the parties.

Lines 125–130 state that prior to acceptance of the offer, the listing broker or the buyer's broker will hold the earnest money. If the offer is not accepted, the earnest money is to be promptly disbursed to the person who paid the earnest money.

Lines 131–138 refer to the procedures for disbursement of earnest money. Earnest money is distributed at closing according to the closing statement or according to a written disbursement agreement signed by all parties to the offer. If the written disbursement agreement hasn't been delivered to the broker within 60 days, the broker may choose from among the various options indicated on lines 133–135. Included in the options is the right to file an interpleader action where the broker places the earnest money in the hands of the court and asks the parties to resolve the dispute over the earnest money. The broker may deduct from the earnest money any legal costs up to $250 prior to disbursement.

Lines 139–146 deal with legal rights and action related to disbursement of earnest money. Lines 139–140 make it clear that the broker's disbursement of earnest money does not determine the legal rights of the parties. The broker is required to send the parties notice of the disbursement at least 30 days prior to the disbursement; if the parties disagree they may take legal action.

Lines 141–143 state that Small Claims Court has jurisdiction over all earnest money disputes involving 1–4 unit residential dwellings.

Lines 147–161 refer to title evidence. The seller is to pay all costs of providing title evidence in the form of either an abstract of title or an owner's policy of title insurance.

Lines 162–165 make clear that the offer reflects the <u>entire</u> agreement of the buyer and the seller.

Lines 164–165 stress that the agreement is binding on parties' heirs as well as estate.

Lines 166–204 provide selected definitions relevant to the offer to purchase. Line 167 states that acceptance occurs when all buyers and sellers have signed the offer. Lines 168–187 identify conditions that might affect the property transaction.

Lines 189–193 deal with how to calculate days when determining deadlines specified in the contract. Deadlines identified as a specific number of "days" from the occurrence of an event are calculated by excluding the day the event occurred; the deadline expires at midnight on the last day.

Lines 194–202 define the term "fixtures"; the list includes new items such as built-in appliances and fences. Lines 203–205 define "time is of the essence." If "time is of the essence" applies to the deadline or date, failure to perform by the exact deadline or date is a breach of contract.

Lines 206–224 identify provisions related to financing. Lines 207–212 deal with responsibilities of the buyer with regard to obtaining a loan commitment. For example, line 208 states that the buyer agrees to apply for financing promptly and to provide evidence of application promptly upon request of the seller.

Lines 213–217 refer to financing unavailability. If the buyer is unable to obtain financing from any lender, the seller has five days to provide the required loan unless a specific loan source was named in the financing contingency.

Lines 218–221 relate to an offer that involves a land contract. Line 221 states that the seller must provide written proof that all creditors whose consent is required have consented to the land contract sale.

Line 222 calls for the property address to be sure that pages 1 and 2 are connected to pages 3 and 4.

Lines 223–224 introduce optional provisions that if marked with an "X" become part of the offer; if unmarked or marked N/A they are not part of the offer.

Lines 225–260 present the optional contingency provisions.

Lines 266–270 define "defect" and line 271 provides for the licensee to include other documents such as an addendum as part of the offer.

Handling Earnest Money Deposits

The subject of commingling funds and the broker's responsibility for the funds of others is described in detail in Chapter 13 of this supplement as part of the rules and regulations enforced by the Real Estate Board. Whenever a real estate broker has monies belonging to another person, the broker must *maintain a separate account in an authorized financial institution for monies belonging to and held for other persons, such as earnest money deposits.*

Risk of Loss

In Wisconsin, the *seller bears any risk of loss that may occur before title passes, as provided in the Uniform Vendor and Purchaser Risk Act*, adopted in 1941.

Statute of Limitations

The time during which parties to a contract may bring legal suit to enforce their rights is limited to *six years* in Wisconsin. Parties who do not take steps to enforce their legal rights within this statute of limitations may lose them.

Land or Installment Contracts

Land contracts, or *installment contracts,* as they are called in the text, frequently are used in Wisconsin. The Wisconsin laws covering the use of land contracts are discussed in Chapter 14/15 of this supplement.

Escrow Closings

Escrow closings as described in the text are seldom used in Wisconsin. *Escrow sometimes is used at the time of closing if the seller has failed to do something that he or she had agreed to do.* Part of the purchase price may be withheld if, for example, the seller has failed to repair a window that has rotted out or has not fixed a broken stair as promised. The part of the purchase price retained is entrusted to an escrow agent. The *escrow agent is a third person, usually an attorney or an officer of the lending institution.* An agreement generally is signed providing that if the work is done on time and to the satisfaction of the buyer, the seller will receive the withheld money.

Escrows now are being used more widely in connection with construction loans in Wisconsin. Agreements of this kind are regulated by the title insurance companies where such escrows are arranged. There are no state regulations for escrows.

QUESTIONS

1. In Wisconsin, licensees may use forms prepared or approved by the Wisconsin

    1. Real Estate Board.
    2. Real Estate License Law.
    3. Department of Natural Resources.
    4. Department of Regulation and Licensing.

2. In Wisconsin, a salesperson may *not* prepare a/an

    1. listing contract.
    2. residential lease.
    3. office lease.
    4. offer to purchase.

3. When a contract depends on its terms being carried out exactly by the date specified, the contract usually contains a/an

    1. time is of the essence clause.
    2. statute of limitations.
    3. extension clause.
    4. equitable title form.

4. Personal property that is to be included in the sale of real estate should be

    1. specified in the sales contract.
    2. sold separately and listed in a separate contract.
    3. conveyed by a warranty deed.
    4. conveyed by a quitclaim deed.

5. Which of the following statements does *not* correctly describe the Marital Property Act?

    1. Title determines ownership rights to property.
    2. Title determines management rights of a property.
    3. Title determines control rights of a property.
    4. Title does not determine ownership rights to a property.

Use the information contained in the offer to purchase contract that appears on pages 37–40 to answer questions 6 through 12.

6. Which of the following statements is true of the property?

   1. It is being purchased by George and Martha Carter.
   2. Legally, it is described as Lot 2, Block 4, Fairmont Subdivision, NW ½ of Section 8, T9N, R7E, Dane County, Wisconsin.
   3. It is being sold by Jay and Linda Jones.
   4. It is being purchased for a sales price of $56,900.

7. Information on an inspection contingency would be placed on which of the following lines on the offer to purchase?

   1. 18–22   3. 168–188
   2. 75–84   4. 256–270

8. According to the offer to purchase, the seller must provide evidence of title to the buyer at the seller's expense at least how long before closing?

   1. 30 days   3. 3 business days
   2. 15 days   4. 15 business days

9. The offer to purchase allows the seller to provide which of the following types of evidence of title to the buyer prior to closing?

   1. Certificate of registration
   2. Certificate of title
   3. Title Insurance
   4. None of the above

10. The buyers are *not* assuming the

   1. sellers' mortgage.
   2. sellers' owners' title insurance policy.
   3. sellers' homeowners' insurance policy.
   4. All of the above are being assumed by the buyers.

11. The transaction will be closed

   1. on or before September 13, 1994.
   2. on or before November 15, 1994.
   3. on or before December 15, 1994.
   4. at the offices of the First Federal Bank of Madison.

11

Transfer of Title

SUCCESSION

The *Wisconsin Law of Intestate Succession* provides that real estate located in Wisconsin owned by a person who has died intestate (without leaving a valid will according to escheat) is to be distributed as follows:

1. The spouse receives the entire estate unless there are children from a previous marriage.

2. If there are children of a prior marriage, the surviving spouse receives one-half of the estate and the remaining one-half of the estate is shared equally by all of the children of the decedent spouse. Classification under the Marital Property Act does not matter because the surviving spouse gets only one-half of the marital property that he or she already owned plus one-half of all of the deceased spouse's other property.

3. If there is neither a surviving spouse nor surviving children, the law lists parents, brothers and sisters, nieces and nephews, grandparents, then other kin as the order in which they are to inherit property.

4. The state school fund receives the property of those who die without heirs.

WILLS

A surviving spouse cannot be excluded totally by a will unless he or she agrees to such exclusion in a written marital agreement. By law, surviving spouses may elect to take up to a one-half interest in property owned by the decedent prior to 1986, which would have been marital property if it had been acquired after 1985. Moreover, a court may award a surviving spouse as much of the estate as necessary for that spouse's support.

If there are assets to be transferred, jointly owned property, survivorship marital property or individually owned life insurance may substitute for a will. Jointly owned property and survivorship marital property automatically are transferred to the survivor; insurance policies can direct that proceeds be paid directly to a beneficiary. One must remember, however, that a will has various important functions, such as naming a guardian for minor children and saving taxes. One may need alternate heirs in case both joint owners, such as both spouses, die together.

Spouses may sign a marital agreement that provides that on the death of either spouse, any or either or both spouses' property will pass without probate to a designated person, trust or other entity. Such a marital agreement, if properly drafted, can be a total will substitute.

This material supplements Chapter 11 in *Modern Real Estate Practice* by Galaty, Allaway and Kyle.

INVOLUNTARY TRANSFER

Adverse Possession

In Wisconsin, legal title may be acquired by adverse possession after *continuous possession of the land for either 10 years or 20 years*, depending on the circumstances. If a *claim of title* is based on a written instrument, such as a deed that later proves faulty, the occupant may claim ownership by *adverse possession* after possessing the land for *ten years*. Possession is established if the land is (1) improved, (2) usually cultivated, (3) enclosed, (4) used to supply fuel or fencing timber or (5) set aside for the ordinary use of the possessor.

In some cases, land that has been improved but is a part of a plot that customarily is not cleared or enclosed also may be claimed. *This might happen when the legal description on a conveyance is incorrect or a surveyor's error causes incorrect boundary lines.* If such errors are discovered after a person has lived on the land for the ten-year prescriptive period, the occupant of the land may claim ownership by adverse possession and will not have to change the boundary lines or move any improvements.

If a claim of adverse possession is *not based on a written instrument*, the prescriptive period is *20 years* and only the premises *actually occupied* can be claimed. Actual occupancy in this circumstance is established if the land has been improved, cultivated or enclosed.

Court action. Court action to defeat a claim by adverse possession must begin within *one year* after interrupting use by the one who is possessing the property and within the prescribed 10-year or 20-year possession period. Any claim by adverse possession, with or without an instrument, must be *open, notorious* and *hostile*.

VOLUNTARY ALIENATION

Deeds

Any deed for the transfer of property in Wisconsin *is valid if it is signed by the grantor, identifies the parties and interest conveyed and is delivered*. The names of all signers must be printed or typed under all signatures. A deed usually is turned over to the grantee at the closing of a real estate transaction. *Title is passed irrevocably when the deed is delivered to the grantee in return for the money.* The deed should be recorded by the grantee as soon as possible after it has been executed. Deeds are recorded at the office of the register of deeds in the county in which the described land is located. An unrecorded deed is still valid between the grantor and grantee. The recording fee usually is paid by the buyer. The subject of recording deeds and other documents is discussed in Chapter 12 of the text and this supplement.

Acknowledgment

As indicated in the text, *any instrument that is to be recorded must be acknowledged or authenticated by a notary public*. In Wisconsin, a notary public is appointed for the state-at-large and may act anywhere in the state. Other officials, including clerks of the court of records, court commissioners, county clerks and deputy clerks, also may acknowledge instruments. An instrument to be recorded also may be authenticated by an attorney.

Real Estate Transfer Fee

Wisconsin does not require a documentary stamp tax, but the state does impose a real estate transfer fee on all conveyances of real estate. The fee is $.30 per $100 of the value of the property or fraction thereof. For example, if the value of the property sold is $30,000, the fee is $90. If the value is

$30,050, the fee is $90.30. The sales price is rounded up to the next $100 and multiplied by .003. The tax applies to the full sales price of the property regardless of any liens or encumbrances that may stand against the property. In addition, as of August 1, 1992, the transfer fee must be paid by the seller (grantor) at the time a land contract is recorded even though the deed will be recorded later. For example, the transfer tax would be $149.70 on a property sold for $49,900 even though there might be a $30,000 mortgage assumed by the buyer.

The transfer fee must be paid by the seller (grantor) to the register of deeds at the time the deed is recorded. A Wisconsin Real Estate Transfer Return form must be submitted at the time the fee is paid and must show the value of the property. Payment of a transfer fee is not required for: (1) conveyances between husband and wife or parent and child for nominal or no consideration, (2) correcting deeds, (3) liquidation deeds, (4) conveyances of real estate with a value of $100 or less and (5) other exemptions, as explained in the text.

Rental Weatherization Requirements

As of January 1, 1985, most residential properties in Wisconsin must meet minimum energy-conservation standards at the time of ownership transfer. Private state-centered inspectors are to be hired by owners to check properties for compliance with the standards. In order to enforce these standards, the statutes prohibit a county register of deeds from recording any transfer of a property that includes a rental dwelling unit unless (1) an inspector has certified the property or (2) the buyer has filed a stipulation to bring the dwelling unit up to code within a year or (3) the property transfer is shown to be excluded from the code or (4) the buyer has filed a statement that the building will be demolished within two years.

The code applies to a building only when its ownership is to be transferred. According to the code, "transfer" means a transfer of ownership by deed, land contract or judgment. In the case of a land contract, transfer occurs when the contract is entered into, not when the deed is transferred. Ownership conveyance also includes transfer of a controlling stock or controlling partnership interest and interest in a lease in excess of one year that was contracted after January 1, 1985.

Excluded from coverage by the code are transfers that are

1.   for security purposes;

2.   between agent and principal or trustee and beneficiary without consideration;

3.   part of a divorce settlement;

4.   for no or nominal consideration between husband and wife or parent and children;

5.   part of the probate process;

6.   involuntary, including foreclosures, bankruptcies and delinquent taxes or assessments; or

7.   to declare a building a condominium.

Only residential rental properties are covered by the code. However, a number of these are excluded, including

1.   seasonal dwelling units not rented any time between November 1 and March 31 each year;

2.   buildings with four units or fewer if the buyer will live in one of the units for at least one year immediately after the transfer;

3. one-family or two-family dwellings constructed under the requirements of ILHR Ch. 22 (effective December 1, 1978) that are less than ten years old;

4. buildings with more than two dwelling units constructed under the requirements of ILHR Ch. 63 (effective April 15, 1976) that are less than ten years old;

5. mobile homes;

6. hotels, motels and tourist rooming houses that are licensed by the Wisconsin Department of Health and Social Services; and

7. hospitals or nursing homes that are licensed by the Wisconsin Department of Health and Social Services.

Buildings subject to the weatherization standards must meet the following requirements in order to be eligible for a certificate of compliance:

1. Insulation must be installed in "accessible" areas to the levels shown in the code. "Accessible" means the space can be reached without removal or alteration of any finishing materials of the permanent structure. For example, enclosed wall cavities are considered inaccessible and do not require insulating.

2. Patio doors and inward-swinging exterior doors must be insulated, double-glazed or equipped with storm doors unless they are provided with vestibules.

3. Windows must be double-glazed or equipped with storm windows. Exempted are windows in doors and furnace rooms.

4. Weather stripping must be installed on exterior doors and windows where cracks exceed $\frac{1}{10}$ inch.

5. Caulking must be applied to exterior joints for the first three stories of the building.

6. Moisture-control ventilation must be installed in attics and crawl spaces at a rate of one square foot of venting per 300 square feet of floor area.

7. Heating equipment and water heaters must be certified by a service technician as being property adjusted in the past six months.

8. Water heaters in vented spaces or basements and crawl spaces that are uninsulated or have insulated ceilings must be insulated with jackets of at least R-5.

9. Showerheads must restrict flow to three gallons per minute.

10. Air conditioners must be covered and effectively sealed from the inside or outside or both during the heating season.

If an owner can show that a specific weatherization measure for a building will take more than five years to achieve payback, the Wisconsin Department of Industry, Labor and Human Relations (DILHR) will issue an exemption from that measure. When an owner files for an exemption, the cost of compliance with such a requirement must be documented and reasonable, within a range of average or typical costs established by DILHR. An application form with a step-by-step payback calculation is available from DILHR. After issuance, the exemption number is transcribed onto the certificate of compliance by the inspector.

Unless a property or transfer is shown to be excluded from the code, a DILHR transfer authorization must accompany the documents of transfer for rental property when the register of deeds is asked to record them. There are three types of transfer authorizations:

1. Certificate of compliance: If a property meets the weatherization standards of the code, it may receive a certificate of compliance that will cover any transfers for the next five years. A certificate can be issued only by an inspector certified by DILHR. Inspectors are paid by building owners at an agreed upon fee, subject to a state-set maximum.

2. Stipulation: The purchaser of a rental property can accept the responsibility for bringing the building into compliance by signing a stipulation, which requires that a certificate of compliance be obtained within one year after transfer. The stipulation form is obtained from DILHR, a DILHR agent or an authorized municipality. The stipulation is submitted for authorization with a fee to DILHR, a DILHR agent or an authorized municipality. A list of DILHR agents is available from DILHR.

3. Waiver: If demolition of a structure is planned within two years of transfer, an owner can apply for a waiver that will allow transfer of the property without meeting the weatherization standards. The waiver form is obtained and submitted in the same manner as the stipulation form described previously.

Before recording the documents of a transfer, proof of an exclusion will be required by the register of deeds to certify the property being transferred is excluded from the code.

The Rental Unit Energy Efficiency Code also provides for penalties for inspectors or owners attempting to evade the requirements of the code. Any inspector falsifying a certificate will have his or her certification revoked by the department and may be required to forfeit not more than $500 per dwelling unit in the rental unit for which the certificate is issued. Any person who offers documents evidencing transfer of ownership for recordation and who, with intent to evade the requirements of the code, falsely states that the property involved does not include a rental unit, may be required to forfeit not more than $500 per dwelling unit in the rental unit being transferred.

For more information on the program, contact:

Wisconsin Department of Industry, Labor and Human Relations
Safety and Buildings Division
Rental Weatherization Unit
P.O. Box 7971
Madison, WI 53707
Telephone: (608) 266-0671

QUESTIONS

1. John James died intestate, leaving a wife and daughter. Under the law of intestate succession, Mrs. James should receive the

    1. first $50,000 plus one-third of the remaining estate.
    2. first $25,000 plus one-half of the remaining estate.
    3. entire estate.
    4. first $25,000 plus one-third of the remaining estate.

2. Which of the following statements does *not* apply to a deed filed in Wisconsin?

    1. The deed must be signed by the grantor and delivered.
    2. The deed should be recorded.
    3. The buyer (grantee) must sign the deed.
    4. The deed must identify the parties involved.

3. Eleanor Roche owned property in joint tenancy with Carmen Renato. Carmen died intestate, leaving only her husband, Raul. The property goes to

   1. Raul, by right of survivorship.
   2. Raul, the husband, as surviving spouse under the law of intestate succession.
   3. Eleanor because she is now a tenant in common.
   4. Eleanor, by right of survivorship as joint tenant.

4. For 25 years, Nora Shelley has lived on a parcel of land in the northern woods of Wisconsin without title to the land. She has had a garden farm on the land and has built a cabin. Nora can claim the land that she has used as her own by

   1. advertising in the local newspaper that she has a claim on the land.
   2. placing a sign on the land indicating that she has a claim on the land.
   3. informing the owners that she has a claim on the land.
   4. filing a claim of ownership by adverse possession.

5. A house in Wisconsin is sold for $45,050. The buyer has a mortgage for $32,000. How much must the seller pay as a real estate transfer fee when the deed is recorded?

   1. $135   3. $39
   2. $39.30   4. $135.30

6. The Rental Weatherization Code is administered by the

   1. Department of Natural Resources.
   2. Real Estate Board.
   3. Department of Industry, Labor and Human Relations.
   4. Department of Regulation and Licensing.

7. Unless a property or transfer is shown to be excluded from the code, a DILHR transfer authorization must accompany the documents of transfer for rental property when the register of deeds is asked to record them. Which of the following would *not* be an acceptable type of transfer authorization?

   1. Waiver
   2. Certificate of occupancy
   3. Stipulation
   4. Certificate of compliance

8. If a property meets the weatherization standards of the code, it may receive a certificate of compliance, which will cover any transfer of the property for the next

   1. year.   3. three years.
   2. two years.   4. five years.

9. Which of the following types of residential rental properties would be covered by the Rental Weatherization Code?

   1. A mobile home
   2. A single-family home to be occupied by the owner for two years after the transfer
   3. A motel licensed by the Wisconsin Department of Health and Social Services
   4. An owner-occupied, four-unit apartment building

10. If an owner can show that a specific weatherization measure for a building will take more than a certain period of time to achieve payback, DILHR will issue an exemption from that measure. The period of time is how many years?

    1. One   3. Three
    2. Two   4. Five

11. The Rental Weatherization Code states that showerheads must restrict flow to how many gallons per minute?

    1. Two   3. Four
    2. Three   4. Five

12

Title Records

RECORDING DOCUMENTS

Any conveyance, instrument or judgment affecting title to or possession of real estate may be recorded. *An instrument must be acknowledged, or authenticated by signature, in order to be eligible for recording.* It then is deposited in the register of deeds' office of the county in which the property is located and the proper fee is paid.

The courts charge a prospective buyer of real estate with *constructive notice*, making him or her responsible for knowing what documents are in the public record concerning the property. *Documents are filed and indexed in the public record according to the grantor's name and the grantee's name.* Recorded documents give constructive notice from the time they are filed with the register of deeds. Recording also establishes the priority of rights.

Deeds in Wisconsin must be signed and acknowledged or authenticated in order to be recorded. The names of all signers must be typed or printed under the signatures and the deed must identify the person who drafted the instrument. Deeds executed after May 8, 1957, must identify the person who drafted the instrument in order to be recorded.

Unrecorded documents, including deeds, are valid between the parties to the transaction; however, they do not protect the rights of such parties against subsequent purchasers or lenders that do not have actual notice of them and cannot learn of them by inspecting the public record. *In order to be valid against subsequent purchasers, all instruments affecting the sale of real estate must be recorded.*

Foreign Language Documents

An instrument must be *written in English* in order to be recorded in Wisconsin. In order to record a foreign language instrument, a *translated duplicate of the instrument* must be attached to the original along with a written authentication of the instrument.

Title Evidence

In most real estate sales transactions that take place in Wisconsin, *the seller is required to furnish evidence of his or her good title to the property that is being sold.* In Wisconsin, *the title abstract*, as described in the text, *is acceptable evidence of title.* This history of recorded documents affecting the title to a parcel of real estate must be examined and evaluated by a real estate attorney, who then prepares his or her opinion of the title or ownership rights.

This material supplements Chapter 12 in *Modern Real Estate Practice* by Galaty, Allaway and Kyle.

Title Insurance

Title insurance commonly is used in most parts of the state because of the preferable protection offered by such policies and the requirements of federal and state loan programs. Title insurance was developed to protect the purchaser and lender against undetected title defects. The title company will defend suits or claims based on items covered in the policy at its own expense. Several forms of title policies are issued; these have been standardized by the American Land Title Association and are known as ALTA forms.

The owner's policy insures the owner's title. The condition of the title is insured as of the date of the policy. As with most title policies, *it insures against such problems as forged documents, improperly delivered deeds and documents executed by incompetent parties.* It does not insure against those items that are listed as exceptions, including the following: defects in the title known to the owner; unrecorded easements, mechanics' liens and other liens, claims or rights; rights of parties in possession not indicated in the public record; encroachments; factors that would be disclosed by an accurate survey and inspection of the property; and governmental regulations, such as zoning requirements, building codes or eminent domain.

The mortgage or loan policy (ALTA or lender's policy) provides coverage that usually is not included in the owner's policy. *It insures the condition of the mortgage for the lender.* All liens against the property are determined to evaluate the priority of the mortgage lien. This policy insures only the lender, not the owner. However, in a sale in which the buyer is financing the purchase with a mortgage, both the owner's and lender's policies can be ordered together and prepared from the same title search. Title insurance cannot be assumed or transferred.

Torrens System

The Torrens system of registering title to real estate has not been adopted in Wisconsin.

Business Opportunity Sales

Every business, no matter how small, must have a place of operation. Whether it is a small, direct-mail sales enterprise operated from the owner's home or a large manufacturing concern with numerous factories and sales offices, the operation of a business involves the use of real estate. Consequently, when a business is sold, the title or lease to real estate used in the business usually is included in the sale. For this reason, *a person who sells or negotiates the sale of businesses for others for a fee is required to be licensed as a real estate broker*; however, salespeople also may use Business Offers (Wisconsin Department of Regulation and Licensing Form 1379).

Chapter 10 of the text and this supplement explain what must be included in a valid real estate sales contract (earnest money agreement or receipt and agreement to purchase). When the sale includes chattel (trade fixtures) and other items of personal property as well as an interest in the real estate, personal property may be listed in the offer to purchase and an additional agreement must be executed by the seller. At the closing of a business sales transaction, *a separate bill of sale should be executed by the seller for all chattel, stock, materials and other items of personal property that are included in the sale.* Personal property should not be listed in the deed.

A license to act as a real estate broker or salesperson does not entitle the licensee to negotiate the sale of an incorporated business where the transfer is to be made by transfer of the controlling common stock; such a transaction requires the license of a security dealer.

Uniform Commercial Code

The Uniform Commercial Code was adopted in Wisconsin in 1965. The sections of the Code that are most applicable to the real estate business concern *bulk transfers*, which are discussed in Article 6, and *security agreements*. The text offers a general discussion of the code, Article 6 and security agreements.

In most businesses, supplies, goods and services constantly are being purchased on credit and paid for periodically as the suppliers submit their bills. *The regulations relating to bulk transfers are designed to protect the creditors of a business from the fraud that may be perpetrated by a business owner who sells the business, including equipment and stock, and then disappears without paying the creditors.* In such a case, the creditors cannot follow the conveyed goods and demand payment from the new owner unless it can be proved that the new owner had actual knowledge of the fraud.

To prevent such a fraud from occurring in the sale of a business, the purchaser should require the seller to execute a *bulk sales affidavit.* This is *a sworn statement listing any liens or unpaid bills that might become liens against the stock, fixtures or furniture included in the sale.* A list of creditors should be included, specifying the amount due to each creditor. In addition, the purchaser must notify each creditor of the pending sale by registered mail at least five days before the sale takes place. The purchaser of a business who fails to obtain a bulk sales affidavit from the seller or fails to give creditors due notice can be held responsible for unpaid invoices, even though he or she paid the seller in good faith for the full value of the items involved.

The section in the Uniform Commercial Code relating to *security agreements*, as described in the text, is applicable in Wisconsin (*see* Chapter 12 of the text).

Lis Pendens

Wisconsin law requires that notice be recorded when filing a suit that may result in a lien or title claim against any property. This notice, called *lis pendens*, gives constructive notice of the action against the property to any person who has or will acquire an interest in the property. Such notice may create a *cloud on the title*, which will prevent conveyance of the property until the suit is settled. (Lis pendens is discussed in Chapter 9 of the text.)

QUESTIONS

1. To be placed in the public record, documents must be

    1. filed under the grantee's name.
    2. filed under the grantor's name.
    3. acknowledged or authenticated.
    4. filed in the tract index.

2. Which of the following statements is true of unrecorded deeds?

    1. They are valid between parties to a transaction.
    2. They are not valid between parties to a transaction.
    3. They protect the rights of subsequent purchasers and lenders.
    4. They protect the grantee against the claims of subsequent purchasers and lenders.

3. In Wisconsin, deeds may be recorded

    1. under the Torrens system of title registration.
    2. in the office of the local zoning administrator.
    3. in the assessor's office.
    4. in the register of deeds office of the county in which the property is located.

4. Which of the following describes foreign language documents in Wisconsin?

    1. May be recorded if they are acknowledged
    2. Must have an English translation attached to the original in order to be recorded
    3. May be recorded as they appear
    4. May be recorded as they appear if they are authenticated

5. Which of the following statements is true of a title abstract?

1. It is acceptable evidence of title in Wisconsin.
2. It commonly is used in many parts of Wisconsin.
3. It proves positively that the holder has title to the property.
4. It protects the purchaser and lender against undetected title defects.

6. Which of the following statements does not correctly describe the Uniform Commercial Code?

1. The code does not cover bulk transfers.
2. The code has been adopted in Wisconsin.
3. The code covers security agreements.
4. The code affects requirements for the sale of a business property, among other things.

13

Real Estate License Laws

WISCONSIN REAL ESTATE LAW

The real estate business in Wisconsin is regulated by the laws contained in Chapters 15 and 452 of the Wisconsin Statutes and by rules and regulations adopted by the Department of Regulation and Licensing and enforced by the Wisconsin Real Estate Board. These rules elaborate on the basic law and provide additional guidelines for Wisconsin real estate licenses. The laws became effective in 1919, the same year the Wisconsin Real Estate Examining Board was established. In 1982, the Real Estate Examining Board became the Real Estate Board.

Assembly Bill 15 redirected the board to its earliest and most important function: discipline of licensees. It placed less emphasis on the board's role and authority for other regulatory functions, and structured those functions under the responsibility of the department. With this new arrangement, the department is totally responsible for the creation and administration of the exam, which essentially reflects current practices. The department also is responsible for issuing and renewing licenses and approving educational programs. The most significant provision gave the department the responsibility for promulgating administrative rules with advice from the board. In addition, the board can prepare a formal dissenting opinion if it strongly disagrees with any proposed rule change. The board retained its current responsibility for discipline of licensees, whereby four members of the profession and three public members decide whether to reprimand a licensee or to limit, suspend or revoke a license, according to due process of law. The board may also fine a licensee.

Who Must Be Licensed (Section 452.03)

Under Section 452.03 of the Wisconsin Statutes, *it is illegal for a person to engage in the real estate business, to advertise or act temporarily as a real estate broker or salesperson without a real estate license.* The penalty for acting as a broker or salesperson without a license or violating any other provision of the real estate law is a fine of up to $1,000 or up to six months' imprisonment or both (Section 452.17).

In addition, a person engaged in the real estate business or acting as a real estate broker or salesperson *may not file a court suit to collect payment for such activities unless that person can prove that he or she was properly licensed at the time the activities or services in question were performed* (Section 452.20).

Definitions

Real estate broker (Section 452.01[1]). A *real estate broker* is defined as any person who, while acting for another person for compensation or the promise of compensation, negotiates or attempts to negotiate a sale, exchange, purchase or rental of an interest or estate in real estate; sale, exchange, purchase or

This material supplements Chapter 13 in *Modern Real Estate Practice* by Galaty, Allaway and Kyle.

rental of any business, its goodwill, inventory, fixtures or an interest therein; or sale, exchange or purchase of a time share.

The word *person* as used throughout the license law refers to an individual, a partnership or a corporation.

Real estate salesperson (Section 452.01[7]). A *real estate salesperson* is defined as any person who is licensed under and associated with a supervising broker and who directly or indirectly represents that broker when performing any of the activities described under the definition of broker.

Time-share salesperson (Section 452.01[9]). A time-share salesperson is defined as any person who is employed by a licensed broker to sell or offer or attempt to negotiate an initial sale or purchase of a time share, but who may not perform any other acts authorized to be performed by a broker or salesperson. A person desiring to act as a time-share salesperson must submit to the department an application for certificate of registration (Section 452.025[1]).

Apprentice salesperson (Chapter RL22). An *apprentice salesperson* is defined as a person who has met all the requirements for the salesperson's license, but who *has not passed the required licensing examination.* An apprentice salesperson is issued a one-year license that allows him or her to perform some of the activities (discussed later in this chapter) of a real estate salesperson.

If an apprentice applicant does not hold a high school diploma, the department will require him or her to pass an examination before issuing an apprentice license.

Cemetery brokers and salespeople (Section 452.02). Since November 1, 1991, the Real Estate Board no longer has any authority relating to the regulation of cemeteries and cemetery salespeople. A real estate broker or salesperson may sell a cemetery lot for another person; however, if the broker or salesperson does so as an employee of a cemetery authority, the broker or salesperson must obtain a separate cemetery salesperson registration from the Wisconsin Department of Regulation and Licensing.

Mortgage bankers (Section RL40.03[4]b). A person is not able to participate as a mortgage banker, loan originator or loan solicitor unless he or she has been issued a certificate of registration from the Wisconsin Department of Regulation and Licensing. The registrant is not required to take the real estate licensing examination. Licensees who receive a fee for finding or negotiating a mortgage would have to register as loan solicitors with the Wisconsin Department of Regulation and Licensing.

Exceptions (Section 452.01[3]). The real estate license law does not apply to the following:

1. Persons who purchase real estate for their own use or who sell, exchange, lease, rent or otherwise dispose of their own real estate (note the exception under broker's definition)

2. Receivers, trustees, administrators, executors, guardians or persons appointed by or acting under the judgment or order for any court

3. Public officers while performing their official duties

4. Banks, savings and loan associations and other designated financial institutions when transacting business within the scope of their corporate powers as provided by law

5. Credit unions or any licensed attorney who, incidental to the general practice of law, negotiates loans secured by real estate mortgages or encumbrances or transfers of real estate

6. Employees of persons engaged in the previously mentioned activities when such employees are engaged in the specific performance of their duties

7.   Janitors, custodians or other persons employed by an owner or a manager of a residential building who show apartments or accept lease applications

8.   Persons who own rental properties, regardless of the number, and who act on their own behalf when renting these properties

9.   Persons registered as mortgage bankers under Section 440.72 who do not engage in the activities of real estate brokers

THE WISCONSIN REAL ESTATE BOARD (SECTIONS 15.07 AND 15.405)

Organization and Members

The Wisconsin Real Estate Board, as now constituted, was created in 1982. Seven members sit on the board, all of whom are appointed by the governor. The law requires that four of the board members be real estate brokers or salespeople licensed in Wisconsin and that three of the members be from the general public, not engaged in any profession regulated by the Wisconsin Department of Regulation and Licensing. The members are paid $25 per day plus expenses when they are working for the board. Each board member serves for a four-year term; the appointments are staggered to avoid expirations occurring at the same time.

Duties and Powers

Each year, the board elects a chairperson, vice-chairperson and secretary from its members. The board advises the department secretary on matters relating to real estate, especially on administrative rules, and has the power to enforce such rules. Generally, these rules clarify the broader provisions of the law and describe more specific requirements for applicants and licensees.

The Department of Regulation and Licensing conducts examinations to determine the competency of real estate license applicants and prepares letters and bulletins for distribution to its licensees. The department also may authorize the revision of real estate study manuals and other research and educational projects for the benefit of its licensees and the protection of the public. The department, with the board's assistance, approves real estate contractual forms.

Roster of Brokers and Salespeople (Sections 440.035[4] and 452.12[4])

The department makes available *a complete printout of the names and addresses of all licensees in the state* of Wisconsin to the public for purchase at cost.

LICENSING PROCEDURE

Applications and Requirements (Section 452.09)

An application for a real estate license must be made on a form provided by the Wisconsin Department of Regulation and Licensing. In addition, every applicant must

1.   be at least 18 years old;

2.   provide proof of competency as reasonably may be required by the department;

3.   provide information on the business or occupation engaged in by the applicant for two years preceding application;

4.   pass the appropriate licensing examination;

5.   furnish proof of having completed the appropriate educational requirement prior to taking the licensing exam;

6.   provide information on the location from which real estate business will be conducted and how this place of business will be designated; and

7.   furnish any additional information required by the department.

Before receiving a new license, applicants who previously were licensed must show proof that they did not engage in real estate activities during the time their licenses were expired.

Broker-Employer's Duty To Check Licensure of Employees

Chapter RL17 states that a broker-employer shall, prior to employing a licensee and at the beginning of each biennial licensure period, determine that each licensee employed by the broker is properly licensed. A broker-employer may not employ an unlicensed person or a person who has failed to file the notice of employment required under Section RL17.04 or the transfer application required by Section RL17.05 to engage in real estate practice for the broker-employer.

Education Requirements (Chapter RL25)

Each applicant for an original salesperson's license must submit to the department proof of attendance at 72 classroom hours of educational programs approved by the department. The department may waive the educational requirement on proof that the applicant has received ten academic credits in real estate or real estate-related law courses at an accredited institution of higher education.

Each applicant for an original broker's license must submit to the department proof of attendance at an additional 36 classroom hours of educational programs approved by the department.

The department may waive the educational requirement on proof that the applicant has received 20 academic credits in real estate or real-estate-related law courses at an accredited institution of higher education, or proof that the applicant is licensed to practice law in Wisconsin. Educational programs must be completed before taking the licensing examination.

Continuing-Education Requirements (Section 452.12[5])

All licensees, except those initially licensed during the current two-year licensure period, are required to attend up to 12 classroom hours of approved educational programs during each biennial renewal period as a condition of renewal. The continuing-education requirement is determined by the Wisconsin Department of Regulation and Licensing in conjunction with the recommendation of the Wisconsin Real Estate Board. In lieu of classroom education, a licensee may take and pass a test-out examination conducted by the department.

Examinations (Section 452.09[3])

The Wisconsin Real Estate licensing examinations for brokers and salespeople are administered by PSI. The national salesperson exam includes a test consisting of 100 questions and covers general principles and practices of real estate that are the same throughout the country; the state part of the salesperson test includes 40 questions on state law and on the rules and regulations enforced by the Wisconsin Real Estate Board. The Special Lesson at the end of this supplement describes the national salesperson test in some detail and suggests ways to prepare for it.

A score of 75 percent or better on *both* the national and state portions is required to pass the salesperson's or broker's examination. If an applicant passes one portion of the salesperson's exam and fails the other portion, the applicant will have the opportunity to retake the failed portion within the following 12 months. If the applicant fails on the retakes, he or she must retake the entire exam. The broker's exam consists of 100 questions covering state laws, rules and regulations, as well as general brokerage principles.

Licensing Corporations and Partnerships (Section 452.12[2])

A corporation or partnership that applies for a real estate broker's license must have at least *one officer or member who has a real estate broker's license*. The competency of applicants for a partnership license must be verified by two members of the partnership; an application for a corporate license must be signed by the president and secretary of the corporation.

A corporation applying for a broker's license must give the department a list of the names and addresses of the officers and directors. In addition, every officer or member of the firm who wishes to engage in real estate activities must hold a real estate license. The department may require information on every officer and member of the firm, including their names, addresses and previous businesses.

Fees

The following fees are applicable to Wisconsin licensees:

- Issuance of an original salesperson license — $ 34
- Issuance of an original broker license — 34
- Renewal fee for a salesperson license — 55
- Renewal fee for a broker license — 74
- Renewal fee for a partnership or corporation license — 46
- Registration of a loan originator — 34
- Renewal fee of a loan originator — 155
- Registration of a loan solicitor — 34
- Renewal fee of a loan solicitor — 210
- Registration of a mortgage banker — 34
- Renewal fee of a mortgage banker — 330
- Late penalty for filing within 30 days of the expiration date — 5
- Late penalty for filing after 30 days following the expiration date — 25
- Transfer to a new employing broker — 5

Issuing a License

An applicant who has passed the appropriate real estate license examination and has complied with the necessary requirements will be granted a license by the department. The license authorizes the new licensee to engage in the activities of a real estate broker or salesperson as described in the license law. Every license shows the name and address of the licensee. Both a wall license and a pocket license are issued to all licensees. Licenses are sent directly to the applicant.

Licensing Nonresidents (Chapter RL20, Section 452.11)

Nonresidents who apply for a license to engage in real estate activities in Wisconsin must fulfill all of the requirements that apply to a resident. As of May 1992, the nonresident broker no longer has to maintain an active place of business in the state in which the person was licensed and is allowed to employ brokers, salespeople or time-share salespeople in Wisconsin.

Irrevocable consent. Before any license can be issued to an applicant, *the applicant or licensee and every resident licensee who becomes a nonresident must file an irrevocable consent form with the department.* This consent provides that actions brought against the out-of-state licensee in connection with real estate transactions in Wisconsin may be initiated in any Wisconsin court of competent jurisdiction. Notice of such suits may be served on the Wisconsin Department of Regulation and Licensing, which will send a duplicate copy to the nonresident licensee. The consent also stipulates that the court's ruling on any suit will be binding on the nonresident licensee.

GENERAL OPERATION OF A REAL ESTATE BUSINESS

Place of Business

Every resident real estate broker must *maintain a definite address in Wisconsin that is used as a principal place of business.* The broker must conduct business only under the name and at the address indicated on his or her license. The department requires a definite address rather than a post office box number; however, a broker can work out of his or her home. *The broker's license must be displayed prominently* in that place of business. It is unlawful for a broker to allow a salesperson to use the broker's license and operate a real estate business in the broker's name if the broker has no control or only nominal control of the business.

Branch Office (Section 452.12)

A broker may establish one or more branch offices, as defined by Wisconsin regulations. All business transacted in the branch office must be performed in the name of the broker-employer and under the direct supervision of a full-time broker-manager.

Each branch office must be managed by a real estate broker employed as a licensed salesperson by the broker-employer or by an officer of a corporation or a partner of a partnership who has a broker's license.

Change of Address (Chapter RL23)

The department must be notified of any change in a licensee's address within 30 days of the change. In such a case, the licensee may make the change on the license or may request a new license and pay a $5 fee. Failure to report a change of address constitutes grounds for revocation or suspension of the broker's license.

License Renewal

Wisconsin real estate licenses are renewed on a biennial basis. Licensees should return the application for renewal in the fall of every *even-numbered year following licensure.* Any licensee who has failed to renew his or her license by *January 1* must cease real estate activities until a new license is issued. Licenses may be renewed within 30 days of the expiration date if the renewal application is accompanied by a late penalty of $5. After 30 days, the penalty is raised to $25.

Termination of Employment

A salesperson may be licensed under only one broker at a time. When a salesperson is discharged or terminated for any reason, the salesperson must send a notice of termination to the department within ten days after the termination of employment.

A salesperson who has terminated employment with a broker may not engage in any real estate activities until a transfer application has been filed with the department. When transferring to a new broker-employer, a salesperson must submit the transfer form with a $5 fee. The license should not be submitted with the form and the fee. The transfer form will register the name of the new broker with the Wisconsin Department of Regulation and Licensing. A form will be sent to the salesperson, with a copy for his or her new broker-employer, stating the name of his or her registered broker-employer. The salesperson can begin working for the new broker as soon as the transfer form is completed and mailed. If the salesperson does not receive the registration slip, he or she should check with the department to be sure it received the transfer form.

Apprentice Salesperson's Activities (Chapter RL22)

Wisconsin regulations severely limit the real estate activities that may be performed by an apprentice salesperson under a temporary license. During the first six months, an apprentice salesperson is not permitted to secure any listing or offer to purchase unless accompanied by a licensed salesperson or broker. All contracts negotiated by the apprentice must be inspected by the employing broker before they are considered legally binding on the parties. *Apprentices are never permitted to conduct closings,* nor can they advertise property or collect commissions on sales. Wisconsin brokers are charged with instructing apprentices in real estate activities for a minimum number of hours each week.

Delivery of Contracts (Chapter RL15)

Wisconsin brokers or salespeople must deliver a copy of every listing agreement, lease, offer to purchase and closing statement to all parties connected with these transactions at the time such documents are signed. In addition, a broker must maintain a copy of all closing statements in his or her files for a period of *three years* from the date of closing.

Care and Handling of Funds (Chapter RL18)

All funds entrusted to a broker in connection with a real estate transaction must be placed in a special trust account that the broker maintains for this purpose in a Wisconsin bank, savings bank, savings and loan association or credit union. A new real estate trust-account law became effective on November 3, 1993. The new law requires that client funds from sales transactions, such as earnest money or other money be held in interest-bearing common trust accounts. The new law defines client funds as all down payments, earnest money deposits or other money related to a conveyance of real estate that is received by a broker, salesperson or time-share salesperson on behalf of the broker's, salesperson's or time-share salesperson's principal or any other person. Promissory notes are not included in the definition of client funds. The new law regarding client funds relates to sales, exchange, and option transactions. Nonclient funds include property management and transactions involving leases.

The interest earned on interest-bearing trust accounts related to client funds will be paid annually by the depository institution to the Wisconsin Department of Administration to assist in the implementation of Wisconsin's program for aiding the homeless.

A broker may establish more than one trust-fund account. The only time a broker must keep a trust account and maintain records is when the broker has real estate trust funds in his or her possession.

The broker must inform the department of the name of the financial institution and the account number under which these funds are deposited. The broker also should notify the department of any changes in this information. *The broker is held personally responsible for all funds* while they are in his or her possession. In general, only the broker can withdraw or deposit funds into a trust account although other persons may sign trust-account checks or share drafts if certain requirements are met.

Special trust-account funds must be deposited within 48 hours of receipt by the broker or salesperson. If money is received prior to a holiday or nonbusiness day, money may be deposited on the next business day. In a few instances, earnest-money deposits will take the form of government bonds, stocks or other nondepositable funds. Chapter RL18 states that nondepositable payments (with the exception of promissory notes) may not be held by a broker as a down payment; nondepositable payments must be held by some other party, subject to an escrow agreement prepared by the parties or an attorney.

Entrusted funds may never be commingled (mixed in) with a real estate licensee's personal funds. A broker is prohibited from depositing any funds in the account that were not received in connection with a real estate transaction for which the broker is acting as agent, except for one or two minor exceptions to the rule. However, a broker may deposit a sum not to exceed $300 from his or her personal funds that is specifically identified and deposited to cover service charges relating to the trust account.

The broker is required to remove commissions, fees and reimbursable expenses from the trust account *within 24 hours after the transaction is consummated* or terminated or after the commissions or fees are earned in accordance with the contract involved.

Revised administrative rules on trust accounts became effective on September 1, 1994, and mandated the following changes.

1. Brokers may have more than one interest-bearing trust account for client funds.

2. Brokers may authorize other persons to sign trust account checks provided only one condition is satisfied: the person must be 18 years of age.

3. Brokers must transfer earnest money to a listing broker no later than 30 days after they receive it, unless they have obtained definitive information from the depository institution that a check has not cleared.

4. Brokers have ten days to increase their personal funds in a trust account to cover a shortage of funds needed to pay service charges.

Record Keeping (Chapter RL18)

A broker is required to keep *specific records* regarding deposits and disbursements of entrusted funds. The broker must have a set of checks and deposit slips for the trust account that indicate the broker's business name and address and clearly identify the account as a real estate trust account. Checks drawn on this account must be identified as to the specific transactions and be retained by the broker along with any voided checks. The broker also must keep a duplicate deposit receipt that shows the source of each deposit and the date and place it was made.

In addition, the broker must keep a *permanent* record book of itemized deposits and disbursements of entrusted funds. For all funds received, the record book must include the date, the names of the parties and the amount. For all disbursements, the journal must include the date, the payee, the check number and the amount. A running balance must be recorded for each day in which receipts or disbursements are entered in the book.

Each broker also must keep an *individual trust ledger sheet* for each transaction, noting the details of the transaction and any entrusted funds taken in or paid out by the broker. For funds received, the ledger must include the names of the parties to a transaction, the date and the amount. For disbursements, the date, the payee, the check number and the amount must be recorded.

A real estate trust-fund account generally must be balanced monthly. All related records must be kept up to date and a *bank reconciliation* prepared. The reconciliation then must be *compared against the journal and the ledger.* Departmental auditors or other representatives may examine and audit the broker's trust-fund account when they deem it necessary.

The new trust-account law states that if brokers have their trust-account records computerized, they must make a backup copy of them on any day in which entries are made. The backup copy must be on a medium that is separate from that on which the source documents reside. Brokers must also be able to immediately print out computer records and make them available to the Department of Regulation and Licensing when requested.

Commissions

As noted earlier, *a person must hold a real estate license to collect a commission* for engaging in real estate activities. In addition, Section 452.19 of the Wisconsin Statutes makes it *illegal for a licensee to split a fee* with someone who does not have a real estate license.

Licensees' Obligations to the General Public (Chapter RL24)

The department has adopted a comprehensive code of ethics. Copies of real estate statutes and rules, which include the code of ethics, may be obtained by writing to:

Wisconsin Department of Regulation and Licensing
Bureau of Direct Licensing and Real Estate
Document Sales Division
P.O. Box 8935
Madison, WI 53708

Current rules relating to the practice of real estate in Wisconsin cost $5.28, which includes tax and handling.

Legal Advice to Licensees (Chapter RL16)

As discussed in Chapter 10, Wisconsin brokers and salespeople may prepare approved preprinted documents relating to real estate transactions. However, a *licensee may prepare documents only for transactions in which he or she is acting as a broker, an agent or a principal.* At no time may a licensee charge a fee for preparing those documents or attempt to explain any of the legal implications of the documents to any party to the transaction.

Advertising (Chapter RL24)

Regulations regarding advertising in real estate are covered in Section 100.18 of the statutes and enforced by the Wisconsin Department of Agriculture, Trade and Consumer Protection. This law includes a section that is meant to protect consumers against unfair, deceptive, false and misleading practices by merchants. It is reasonably clear that the broker is considered a merchant in a transaction involving real estate.

Chapter RL24.04 requires licensees to *present a true picture* when advertising or making representations to the public. Licensees may not *advertise without disclosing the licensee's name* or permit any person associated with the licensee to use individual names or telephone numbers unless such person's connection with the licensee is obvious in the ad.

"For sale" signs. Wisconsin has no state regulations regarding "for sale" signs, although some municipalities in the state have either limited the use of signs or prohibited them altogether.

SUSPENSION OR REVOCATION OF A LICENSE (SECTION 452.14)

The department may investigate the actions of any licensee who is suspected of performing one or more prohibited acts while engaging in real estate activities.

The investigation may be instigated solely by the department or it may be prompted by the written complaint of any person claiming to have been injured or defrauded by the actions of a real estate licensee. A licensee may be disciplined for any of the following acts:

1. Making a material misstatement

2. Making a substantial misrepresentation

3. Making false promises

4. Pursuing a continued course of misrepresentation through agents, salespeople or advertising

5. Acting for more than one party in a transaction without informing all parties

6. Accepting a commission or referral fee as a salesperson from any person except the employer

7. Representing or attempting to represent a broker other than his or her employer, without the express knowledge and consent of the employer

8. Failing to account for or pay out any monies belonging to others that have come into the licensee's possession

9. Displaying any conduct that demonstrates incompetency

10. Paying or offering to pay a commission to anyone who does not hold a real estate license

11. Intentionally encouraging or discouraging any person from purchasing or renting real estate in a particular area on the basis of race

12. Being guilty of any other conduct that constitutes improper, fraudulent or dishonest dealing

13. Violating any provision of Chapter 452 of the Wisconsin Statutes or of the department's rules and regulations

14. Failing to use forms approved by the department

15. Treating unequally any person solely because of sex, race, color, handicap, religion, sexual orientation, national origin, ancestry, marital status, lawful source of income or familial status or in any other unlawful manner

In addition to the above discipline, the board may assess a forfeiture of not more than $1,000 for each violation and require additional education or training.

Right to a Hearing

The department *cannot suspend or revoke a license of any licensee without offering the licensee a right to a public hearing.* At least *ten days* before the hearing, the board must send written notice of the time and place of the hearing to the applicant or licensee and to his or her attorney.

A real estate broker or salesperson who is notified that his or her license is suspended or revoked immediately must forward the license to the department. A broker's license issued to a corporation or a partnership may be suspended if a licensed officer, partner or director commits an action sufficient to cause suspension or revocation.

Restraining Orders (Section 452.16)

If the department feels that a person is acting without a license and that this activity might be injurious to the public interest, the department may petition the circuit court for a *temporary restraining order, injunction* or *writ of ne exeat* against a licensee in lieu of a hearing.

Review (Chapter 227)

A person whose real estate license has been *limited, suspended or revoked*, or who has been reprimanded by the board, has a right to *request a review by the circuit court of the county in which the licensee resides.* The court will review the proceedings at which the disciplinary action took place.

Reissue of Licenses (Section 452.15)

A licensee whose license is revoked or denied may not reapply for licensure until the expiration of a period determined in each case by the board, or in the case of a second offense of racial discrimination, not less than five years from the date the revocation became finally effective.

QUESTIONS

1. Which of the following persons must have a real estate broker's license in order to transact business?

   1. Wilfred Shannon, who owns a six-flat and personally manages the building, collects rent and shows the apartments to prospective tenants
   2. Leslie Albers, who negotiates the sale of entire business, including their stock, equipment and buildings, for a promised fee
   3. Frank Drew, superintendent of a large apartment building, who shows apartments to prospective tenants as part of his regular duties
   4. Wanda Sutton, who has her father's written authority to negotiate the sale of and to convey a residence he owns

2. The Wisconsin Real Estate Board is composed of

   1. five members, who are real estate brokers licensed in Wisconsin.
   2. six members, who are real estate brokers licensed in Wisconsin.
   3. four members, who are real estate brokers or salespeople licensed in Wisconsin, and three public members.
   4. seven members, who are real estate brokers or salespeople licensed in Wisconsin, and three public members.

3. Applicants for a real estate salesperson's license must

   1. be at least 19 years of age.
   2. complete 30 credits in real estate before being issued a license.
   3. be at least 21 years of age.
   4. complete the appropriate educational requirement prior to taking the licensing exam.

4. Wisconsin real estate law requires that persons applying for a broker's license must attend how many classroom hours of educational programs approved by the department?

    1. 45   3. 90
    2. 72   4. 108

5. Which of the following statements regarding the licensing of corporations and partnerships as real estate brokers is true?

    1. All the officers or partners must qualify as brokers and pass the required written examination.
    2. The corporation's or partnership's license is in effect only as long as the designated broker is associated with the firm.
    3. Any partner or officer of a licensed corporation may engage in brokerage activities.
    4. The applicant corporation or partnership must file an irrevocable consent agreement with the commission.

6. Which of the following statements does *not* correctly describe a branch office?

    1. A branch office must operate under the same name as the parent office.
    2. A branch office must have a manager who is a licensed real estate broker.
    3. A broker may establish no more than ten branch offices.
    4. All business transacted in the branch office must be performed in the name of the broker-employer.

7. When a salesperson is discharged or terminated for any reason, the supervising broker

    1. must send a letter of release to the department.
    2. must send a communication to the salesperson's last known residence informing the salesperson that his or her license has been returned to the board.
    3. must state whether the person was competent.
    4. is not responsible for informing the department of the discharge or termination.

8. An earnest-money deposit received by the broker must be

    1. placed in the broker's business account.
    2. given to the seller within 24 hours.
    3. kept in an office safe with proper records maintained by the broker.
    4. deposited in a special trust account within 48 hours after the broker receives it.

9. Salesperson Omar Kent is unhappy with the terms of his association with the Sara Holmes Realty Company and has decided to associate with Jerry Curtis at Curtis Homes. Before Kent can begin selling for Curtis

    1. Sara Holmes must send Kent's pocket license to Curtis.
    2. Curtis must notify the department of the change.
    3. Kent must file a transfer application form with the department.
    4. Sara Holmes must return Kent's pocket license to the commission.

10. Which of the following is *not* cause for the revocation of a real estate license in Wisconsin?

    1. Paying a commission to a person who does not hold a real estate license
    2. Selling cemetery plots without holding a Wisconsin real estate license
    3. Posting a For Sale sign without the consent of the owner
    4. Representing anyone other than a salesperson's supervising broker without the consent of that broker

11. Which of the following statements does not correctly describe what an apprentice salesperson may never do during an apprenticeship?

    1. The apprentice may never conduct a closing.
    2. The apprentice may never negotiate a contract without the direct supervision of a licensed salesperson or broker.
    3. The apprentice may never collect commissions on sales.
    4. The apprentice may never advertise property.

12. Which of the following describes the Wisconsin continuing-education requirement?

    1. Applies only to salespeople
    2. Applies only to brokers
    3. Requires all licensees to complete up to 20 hours in approved education programs during each biennial renewal period
    4. Applies to salespeople and brokers

13. Which of the following statements is true of real estate licenses in Wisconsin?

    1. They must be renewed by December 31 of each year following licensure.
    2. They must be renewed by December 31 of every even-numbered year following licensure.
    3. They must be renewed by January 31 of every odd-numbered year following licensure.
    4. They entitle the holder to negotiate a loan secured by real estate.

14. Which of the following does *not* correctly describe what a corporation must do in order to receive a license?

    1. Have one officer or member who has a broker's license
    2. Submit a statement from the corporation president and secretary swearing to the competency of the applicant
    3. Give the department a list of names and addresses of the officers and directors
    4. Prove that every officer of the corporation who will engage in real estate activity for the firm holds a broker's license

15. In order to keep proper records of all real estate transaction funds, a broker must

    1. keep a permanent record book of all deposits and withdrawals, including dates, names and amounts of receipts and disbursals.
    2. keep a separate trust account for each account and not commingle the funds of any two accounts.
    3. place all deposits in a business account.
    4. balance the trust-fund account on a daily basis.

16. Which of the following is true of a broker, under Wisconsin law?

    1. Must maintain a copy of all closing statements for two years from the date of closing
    2. May explain the legal implications of a contract to any party
    3. May not advertise services as free
    4. Must maintain a definite address in the state

17. Which of the following statements is true of Wisconsin real estate licensees?

    1. They must deliver a copy of every contract to the involved parties.
    2. They may, after collecting the fee from the principal, split this fee with any person who has been instrumental in the successful completion of the sale.
    3. They may charge a fee for preparing listing contracts.
    4. They may explain the legal implications of a document to any party.

18. A broker may deposit a sum of money not to exceed a certain amount from her personal funds that is specifically identified and deposited to cover service charges relating to the trust account. The amount of money is

    1. $100.   3. $300.
    2. $200.   4. $400.

19. Which of the following persons would *not* have to have a real estate license in order to transact business?

    1. A business opportunity broker
    2. A time-share broker
    3. A real estate salesperson
    4. A time-share salesperson

20. Which of the following is true of a nonresident broker?

    1. Must maintain an active place of business in the state in which the person is licensed
    2. May employ brokers in Wisconsin
    3. Must file with the department an irrevocable consent form
    4. May not employ time-share salespeople in Wisconsin

21. A broker having to increase her personal funds in a trust account to cover a shortage of funds needed to pay service charges must do so within

    1. 24 hours.
    2. 48 hours.
    3. 5 days
    4. 10 days

Real Estate Financing

MORTGAGES

Wisconsin is a *lien-theory state* with regard to mortgages. According to this theory, a mortgage creates a lien on real property but does not convey title to the property to the mortgagee (lender).

Mortgage Loan Instruments

The two instruments—the mortgage and the note—executed in connection with a mortgage loan are described in the text. The *mortgage* conveys an interest in the real estate to the lender as security for the debt, while the mortgage *note* is a promise to repay the debt. Mortgages are the most common form of loan instruments in Wisconsin. *Trust deeds,* as described in the text, are used in Wisconsin as security for mortgage bond issues for major construction projects only where substantial sums of money are involved.

In Wisconsin, mortgage agreements completed by Wisconsin brokers must be made on forms approved by the *Wisconsin Department of Regulation and Licensing* or the *Wisconsin State Bar Association.* If the department's approval is withdrawn, the form no longer can be used. Several mortgage document forms have been prepared by the State Bar and approved by the department for use by real estate brokers in Wisconsin. The most commonly used is Form 6-L, which appears at the end of this chapter. An attorney should prepare or at least review a mortgage before it is executed.

Mortgage Foreclosure

Most mortgages are foreclosed under *judicial foreclosure by sale,* as discussed in the text. Nonjudicial foreclosure under a power-of-sale clause is permitted in Wisconsin, but is seldom used. *Strict foreclosure,* as discussed in the text, is *not allowed when a mortgage is foreclosed.* It is, however, used for land contracts.

In addition to the procedures previously discussed, a defaulted Wisconsin borrower may settle with the lender on a voluntary, out-of-court basis. If the two parties come to an agreement, the lender may execute a satisfaction of mortgage to the borrower. When the satisfaction is recorded along with a deed to the property executed by the borrower to the lender, the title passes to the lender and the borrower is released from his or her debt. When the parties close out a defaulted mortgage in this manner, Wisconsin courts place a heavy burden of *responsibility on the lender to ensure fair treatment of the creditor.* If a suit is filed, the borrower may be granted the right to redeem the property if he or she can prove unfair treatment.

This material supplements Chapters 14 and 15 in *Modern Real Estate Practice* by Galaty, Allaway and Kyle.

Redemption

A defaulted Wisconsin borrower has the *equitable right of redemption prior to the sale.* Wisconsin statutes allow a *one-year redemption period from the time the foreclosure judgment is entered* (at least 20 days after the action is begun). There is *no statutory redemption (period) after the sale.* Some mortgages, such as those that contain a waiver of deficiency judgment and give the lender the right to appoint a receiver, allow only a six-month equitable redemption period.

Wisconsin Mortgage Provisions

Insurance. Lenders in Wisconsin may *designate the insurance company* that will insure the premises during the time specified on the mortgage document (usually State Bar Form 15). Lenders also may request that they receive duplicate premium notices from the insurance company so that they can be sure that the borrowers are fulfilling their end of the agreement.

Taxes. Form 15 expressly states that *the borrower has the obligation to pay real estate taxes on the mortgaged property.* If the borrower does not pay the taxes, *the lender may pay the taxes and add the expense to the mortgage debt.* A lender might take such an action in order to avoid a superior lien (a tax lien) on the property.

Assignment of Mortgage

In Wisconsin, a mortgage may be sold by a lender to a third party, called an *assignee.* The lender should execute an *assignment of mortgage form* (usually State Bar Form 14), which should be recorded in the office of the register of deeds in the county in which the land is located. The *assignee has exactly the same rights that the original lender had in relation to the borrower.* An assignee should insist that a lender sign his or her name on the back of the mortgage note. This prevents the lender from claiming payments that might be paid to the lender by the borrower. The *assignee should notify the borrower in writing to make payments directly to the assignee.*

Usury

The main features of the Wisconsin usury law that relate to mortgage credit include:

1. Residential mortgage loans covering first-lien mortgages on one-family to four-family dwellings used by borrowers as their principal places of residence can continue to be made without regard to an interest-rate ceiling.

2. A lender may charge a prepayment penalty on a fixed-rate mortgage loan equal to 60 days' interest if that loan is prepaid during the first five loan years.

3. Existing Wisconsin law requiring the refund of unearned interest on prepayment of a mortgage loan is retained; however, for purposes of computing this refund, interest does not include such items as loan-commitment fees and separate charges for services incidental to the loan paid to third parties.

4. A late-payment charge may be imposed by a lender, which is not to exceed 5 percent of the unpaid amount of any installment not paid on or before the 15th day after its due date.

5. All depository lenders will be required to pay 5.25 percent interest on escrows for payment of taxes or insurance on loans originated after January 31, 1983.

6. The residential mortgage lending section does not apply to FHA-insured or VA-guaranteed mortgage loans or loans made to corporations.

Figure 14/15.1   Mortgage

DOCUMENT NO.	State Bar of Wisconsin Form 6-L — 1982 **MORTGAGE** (To be used for: loans over $25,000; loans $25,000 or less and first lien; or other non-consumer act transactions)	THIS SPACE RESERVED FOR RECORDING DATA

Brian O. Regas and Lisa M. Regas, Husband and
wife
_____ ("Mortgagor," whether one or more)
mortgages to First Wisconsin Savings and Loan

_____ ("Mortgagee," whether one or more)
to secure payment of One Hundred Thousand and no/100----------
_____ Dollars ($ 100,000.00)
evidenced by a note or notes bearing an even date executed by _____
Brian O. Regas and Lisa M. Regas _____ to
Mortgagee, and any extensions, and renewals and modifications of the note(s)
and refinancings of any such indebtedness on any terms whatsoever (including
increases in interest) and the payment of all other sums, with interest, advanced
to protect the security of this Mortgage, the following property, together with the
rents, profits, fixtures and other appurtenant interests (all called "Property"),
in   Dane   County, State of Wisconsin:

RETURN TO

Tax Parcel No.: _____

Lot six (6), Block Four (4), Fairmont Subdivision,
in the city of Madison, Dane County, Wisconsin

1. This   is   homestead property.
       (is)   (is not)

2. This   is not   a purchase money mortgage.
       (is)   (is not)

3. MORTGAGOR'S COVENANTS.
   (a) COVENANT OF TITLE. Mortgagor warrants title to the Property, except restrictions and easements of record,
if any and except _____ .

   (b) TAXES. Mortgagor promises to pay when due all taxes and assessments levied on the Property or upon
Mortgagee's interest in it and to deliver to Mortgagee on demand receipts showing such payment.
   (c) INSURANCE. Mortgagor shall keep the improvements on the Property insured against a loss or damage
occasioned by fire, extended coverage perils and such other hazards as Mortgagee may require, through insurers
approved by Mortgagee in such amounts as Mortgagee shall require, but Mortgagee shall not require coverage in an
amount more than the balance of the debt without co-insurance, and Mortgagor shall pay the premiums when due. The
policies shall contain the standard mortgage clause in favor of Mortgagee and, unless Mortgagee otherwise agrees in
writing, the original of all policies covering the property shall be deposited with Mortgagee. Mortgagor shall promptly
give notice of loss to insurance companies and Mortgagee. Unless Mortgagor and Mortgagee otherwise agree in writing,
insurance proceeds shall be applied to restoration or repair of the Property damaged, provided the Mortgagee deems the
restoration or repair to be economically feasible.
   (d) OTHER COVENANTS. Mortgagor covenants not to commit waste nor suffer waste to be committed on the
Property, to keep the Property in good condition and repair, to keep the Property free from liens superior to the lien of this
Mortgage, and to comply with all laws ordinances and regulations affecting the Property. Mortgagor shall pay when due
all indebtedness which may be or become secured at any time by a mortgage or other lien on the Property superior to this
Mortgage and any failure to do so shall constitute a default under this Mortgage.
   4. DEFAULT AND REMEDIES. Mortgagor agrees that time is of the essence with respect to payment of principal
and interest when due and in the performance of any of the covenants and promises of the Mortgagor contained herein or
in the note(s) secured hereby. In the event of default, Mortgagee may, at his option and subject to the notice provisions of
this Mortgage, declare the whole amount of the unpaid principal and accrued interest due and payable and collect it in a
suit at law or by foreclosure of this Mortgage by action or advertisement and the exercise of any other remedy available
at law or equity, and Mortgagee may sell the Property at public sale and give deeds of conveyance to the purchasers
pursuant to the statutes.
   5. NOTICE. Unless otherwise provided in the note(s) secured by this Mortgage, prior to any acceleration (other than
under paragraph 12) Mortgagee shall mail notice to Mortgagor specifying: (a) the default; (b) the action required to cure
the default; (c) a date, not less than 15 days from the date the notice is mailed to Mortgagor by which date the default must
be cured; and (d) that failure to cure the default on or before the date specified in the notice may result in acceleration.
   6. EXPENSES AND ATTORNEY'S FEES. In case of default, whether abated or not, all costs and expenses
including reasonable attorneys' fees and expenses of title evidence to the extent not prohibited by law shall be added to
the principal, become due as incurred, and in the event of foreclosure, be included in the judgment.

MORTGAGE — STATE BAR OF WISCONSIN — FORM 6-L (1982)

Wisconsin Legal Blank Co., Inc.
Milwaukee, Wisconsin

Figure 14/15.1   Mortgage (continued)

7. FORECLOSURE WITHOUT DEFICIENCY. Mortgagor agrees to the provisions of Section 846.101 and 846.103(2) of the Wisconsin Statutes, as may apply to the property and as may be amended, permitting Mortgagee in the event of foreclosure to waive the right to judgment for deficiency and to hold the foreclosure sale within the time provided in such applicable Section.

8. LIMITATION ON PERSONAL LIABILITY. Unless a Mortgagor is obligated on the note or notes secured by this Mortgage, the Mortgagor shall not be liable for any breach of covenants contained in this Mortgage.

9. RECEIVER. Upon default or during the pendency of any action to foreclose this Mortgage, Mortgagor consents to the appointment of a receiver of the Property, including homestead interest, to collect the rents, issues, and profits of the Property, during the pendency of such an action, and such rents, issues, and profits when so collected, shall be held and applied as the court shall direct.

10. WAIVER. Mortgagee may waive any default without waiving any other subsequent or prior default by Mortgagor.

11. MORTGAGEE MAY CURE DEFAULTS. In the event of any default by Mortgagor of any kind under this Mortgage or any note(s) secured by this Mortgage, Mortgagee may cure the default and all sums paid by Mortgagee for such purpose shall immediately be repaid by Mortgagor with interest at the rate then in effect under the note secured by this Mortgagee and shall constitute a lien upon the Property.

12. CONSENT REQUIRED FOR TRANSFER. Mortgagor shall not transfer, sell or convey any legal or equitable interest in the Property (by deed, land contract, option, long-term lease or in any other way) without the prior written consent of Mortgagee, unless either the indebtedness secured by this Mortgage is first paid in full or the interest conveyed is a mortgage or other security interest in the Property, subordinate to the lien of this Mortgage. The entire indebtedness under the note(s) secured by this Mortgage shall become due and payable in full, at the option of Mortgagee without notice, upon any transfer, sale or conveyance made in violation of this paragraph.

13. ASSIGNMENT OF RENTS. Mortgagor hereby transfers and assigns absolutely to Mortgagee, as additional security, all rents, issues and profits which become or remain due (under any form of agreement for use or occupancy of the Property or any portion thereof), or which were previously collected and remain subject to Mortgagor's control, following any default under this Mortgage or the note(s) secured hereby and delivery of notice of exercise of this assignment by Mortgagee to the tenant or other user(s) of the Property. This assignment shall be enforceable with or without appointment of a receiver and regardless of Mortgagee's lack of possession of the Property.

Dated this _____17th_____ day of __April__ , 19_93_.

_Brian O. Regas_____(SEAL)   _Lisa M. Regas_____(SEAL)
　　(Mortgagor)　　　　　　　　　　　　(Mortgagor)
* _____   * _____

_____(SEAL)   _____(SEAL)
　　(Mortgagor)　　　　　　　　　　　　(Mortgagor)
* _____   * _____

AUTHENTICATION

Signature(s) _____

_____

authenticated this _____ day of _____ , 19____

_____

* _____

TITLE: MEMBER STATE BAR OF WISCONSIN
(If not, _____
authorized by Sec. 706.06, Wis. Stats.)

THIS INSTRUMENT WAS DRAFTED BY

_____Edward I. Jones_____

_____

(Signatures may be authenticated or acknowledged. Both are not necessary.)

ACKNOWLEDGMENT

STATE OF WISCONSIN
_Dane_____ County. } ss.

Personally came before me this ____17th__ day of
_April_____ , 19_93_ the above named
Brian O. Regas and Lisa M. Regas,
Individually and as Husband and wife
_____
_____
to me known to be the person _____ who executed the foregoing instrument and acknowledge the same.

_____

* _Edward I. Jones_____

Notary Public _____Dane_____ County, Wis.
My commission is permanent. (If not, state expiration date: _____ March 15_____ , 19_95_.)

*Names of persons signing in any capacity should be typed or printed below their signatures.

7. Lenders violating the residential mortgage sections may be liable to a borrower for $500 plus actual damages, costs and reasonable attorney fees; however, this liability does not apply to cases of unintentional mistakes corrected by the lender on demand.

8. Section 138.056 of the new usury statutes provides for a greatly expanded framework for Wisconsin lenders to make variable-rate mortgage loans.

9. The new Wisconsin law specifically rejects the federal rate ceiling preemption statute enacted in April 1980. However, under the operation of Wisconsin's new law, the need for the federal preemption is eliminated.

Prepayment

In Wisconsin, prepayment penalties may be charged on conventional loans and land contracts, but not on FHA or VA loans.

Wisconsin State Veterans Home-Loan Programs

Wisconsin is one of five states in the country to have a first-mortgage home-loan program for veterans.

A law passed in 1974 allowed the state and the Wisconsin Department of Veterans Affairs to create funds by issuing bonds. The funds provided by these bonds are available for the purchase or construction of private housing with a minimal down payment. A first-mortgage loan, with an annual percentage rate determined by the cost of bonds sold to finance the program, is obtained through a local lending agency. The loan first must be approved by the Wisconsin Department of Veterans Affairs.

Loans are available for the purchase of existing housing (including condominiums) and for the construction of a home as well as the acquisition of land for the construction of a home. The maximum first-mortgage home loan is 95 percent of the total cost. The minimum down payment is 5 percent of the total cost, with a maximum repayment term of 30 years. The 5 percent down payment, as well as closing costs, must be made by the veteran with the veteran's own unborrowed funds, although gifted funds are acceptable. Two and one-half times the amount of the annual income of the veteran and spouse must equal or exceed the amount of the mortgage, or two times the income must equal or exceed the cost of the home and garage only, whichever the veteran elects. The combined annual income of the veteran and spouse may not exceed $47,500, although income limits are not applicable to qualified veterans.

Eligibility is limited to Wisconsin veterans or any other eligible person. The borrower is required to be a resident of Wisconsin and the home must be located in Wisconsin. A veteran or any other eligible person must contact a county veterans service officer to obtain a certificate of eligibility prior to making application for a loan. The home must be occupied by the veteran and his or her family as their principal residence and must be adequately insured for the term of the loan. If mortgage cancellation insurance is used, it must be obtained at the veteran's expense.

Because of a number of recent and pending changes in state and federal law, this first-mortgage program is changing rapidly. Licensees should consult lenders in their area who are authorized to originate loans for the Wisconsin Department of Veterans Affairs to check current requirements for eligibility for these loans.

For more information on the program, call (608) 266-1311.

Veterans Home Improvement Loan Program (HILP)

Wisconsin veterans also are eligible for a home improvement loan of up to $15,000 *at either a 6 or 7.95 annual percentage rate* depending upon the loan the veteran choose. The general conditions relating to this program are similar in many respects to the first-mortgage home-loan program.

Wisconsin Home Program

Created by the legislature in April 1982, this program is designed to help middle-income and low-income people purchase homes by lowering the interest rate that they must pay. This is accomplished by diverting investors' money from other financial instruments to home loans.

Funds for the program are produced by bonds sold by the Wisconsin Housing and Economic Development Authority (WHEDA). Investors buy the bonds because their interest is exempt from federal tax. The bonds, in turn, are able to carry a lower interest rate.

To obtain a loan under the program, buyers must contact a lender authorized to make loans in the program, including banks, savings and loan associations, credit unions and mortgage banks.

WHEDA uses its funds to buy loans from the lenders and guarantee repayment. The authority repays bond-holders with the payments from the home buyers. WHEDA administers the program.

Home buyers are required to make a 5 percent down payment on the loans. Loan terms range from 15 to 30 years. In addition, limits are imposed on the buyer's income and the home's cost. Annual gross income cannot exceed approximately 90 percent of the median income in the buyer's home county. Loans also are available for the purchase of homes in a "target area" or homes that are part of a rehabilitation project. A target area is either in chronic economic distress or has been designated by HUD as eligible for the program. The price of a home cannot exceed a maximum price, which varies from county to county.

For more information on the program, call 1-800-334-6873 toll-free.

Wisconsin Home Improvement Loan Program

This program, administered by WHEDA, was designed to enable low-income and moderate-income homeowners to repair and upgrade their properties and install energy-conserving improvements. The WHEDA program provides FHA-insured home improvement loans at below-market interest rates through participating lending institutions.

The financing for these lower-interest-rate home improvement loans is through the sale of tax-exempt bonds. To apply for a loan, a borrower goes to a participating lending institution, which processes the loan and closes it in the lender's name. Loans are originated and closed by participating lenders at the Housing and Neighborhood Conservation Program (HNCP) interest rate, sent to WHEDA for certification and purchase. WHEDA then sends funds to the lender for disbursement to the borrower. The lender's responsibility ends with the disbursement of the proceeds of the loan; servicing is WHEDA's responsibility.

For more information, call the HNCP, toll-free, at 1-800-334-6873.

Financing Legislation

Consumer protection in financing arrangements within Wisconsin is provided by the federal Truth-in-Lending Act, which applies to real estate transactions, and by the *Wisconsin Consumer Act* and its amendment, *Chapter 428 of the Wisconsin Statutes*.

The Wisconsin Consumer Act is aimed primarily at the regulation of consumer-credit financing of durable goods such as household appliances. *However, the act does include both real and personal property in its definition of a consumer-credit transaction.* Real estate licensees should be aware of its possible effect on real estate sales, *especially on land contract sales.*

Two exemptions to the Wisconsin Consumer Act deal with real estate. The first *exempts consumer-credit transactions in which the amount financed or the base price is more than $25,000.* The second, added by amendment in 1973, *exempts first-mortgage loans in which the amount financed is $25,000 or less and the interest rate is 12 percent or less.* In other words, the provisions of the Consumer Act apply only to junior mortgage loans of $25,000 or less. Although most Wisconsin real estate transactions are exempt from the Consumer Act, the act may have a significant effect on transactions involving land contracts. This effect will be discussed later in this chapter.

LAND CONTRACTS

The land contract, as discussed in the text, often is used in financing real estate in Wisconsin.

Recording the Land Contract

To protect his or her interests, the buyer in a land contract sale should *record the contract with the register of deeds* in the county in which the land is located. *Recording fees usually are paid by the buyer.* As with a mortgage, the land contract must be acknowledged properly. No witnesses are necessary for recording or for the validity of the contract. If the property is the sellers' homestead, both spouses must sign. The signers' names should be typed or printed under their signatures and the name of the person who drafted the instrument must be indicated clearly on the contract.

Land Contract Forms

Only forms approved by the Wisconsin Department of Regulation and Licensing or the Wisconsin State Bar Association may be used by brokers for land contracts in Wisconsin. State Bar Form 11 is designated as the approved form in transactions that are not subject to the Wisconsin Consumer Act. In cases where a land contract is or may be subject to the Consumer Act, State Bar Form 10 should be used.

Impact of the Wisconsin Consumer Act on Land Contracts

Although the Wisconsin Consumer Act does not mention land contracts specifically under its provisions, it may be applicable under certain circumstances. If a seller under a land contract is in the business of regularly advertising property "to induce a consumer transaction," he or she may be under the dictates of the Consumer Act.

The act may

1. prevent the buyer from using his or her *equity interest* in the parcel as security in the purchase of another parcel;

2. prevent the seller from denying the buyer *prepayment privileges*;

3. prohibit *balloon payments* (described in Chapter 15 of the text); and

4. undercut the seller's usual land contract remedies in case of default by *limiting the use of acceleration clauses.*

Assignment of a Land Contract

Nonassignment clauses, which prohibit the transfer of the buyer's interest without the seller's consent, are included in the approved land contract forms in Wisconsin. If there is no such clause in a land contract or if the seller consents, the buyer may transfer his or her interest in the real estate to another. The assignment should be *signed by the parties, acknowledged and recorded.* Assignment of a land contract should be treated in the same manner as any other real estate transaction.

Forfeiture of a Land Contract

Under a land contract containing an *acceleration clause,* a seller may sue a *buyer for the money owed and may obtain a money judgment if the buyer defaults on even one installment.* Although acceleration clauses may be prohibited in land contract transactions that are covered by the Wisconsin Consumer Act, many land contract sales are not covered by the act.

A seller under a land contract also may sue the defaulted borrower for judicial foreclosure. As with a mortgage, the seller may sue the borrower in court to obtain a judgment against the borrower for the entire sum of the loan balance. If the judgment is granted, the judge will establish a redemption period during which the borrower may pay the balance and claim the property. This period is usually shorter than the one-year mortgage redemption period. After the redemption period, the property is sold by the sheriff at public auction. If the proceeds from the sale are insufficient to meet the unpaid debt, the seller may apply for a deficiency judgment against the borrower.

In Wisconsin, a land contract also may be foreclosed by *strict foreclosure.* Under this procedure, the seller sues for foreclosure in court in the manner previously described. However, if the borrower fails to reclaim the property at the end of the redemption period, the seller *receives title to the property* rather than having the property sold at auction. In this case, the lender *cannot apply for a deficiency judgment against the borrower.*

Because land contracts have a shorter redemption period than mortgages and, in the case of strict foreclosure, the seller/lender regains title to the property, land contracts offer sellers certain advantages over mortgages.

QUESTIONS

1. With regard to mortgage loans, Wisconsin is what type of state?

   1. Lien-theory
   2. Title-theory
   3. Intermediate-theory
   4. Combination of lien-theory and title-theory

2. The general remedy on a defaulted mortgage is

   1. a nonjudicial foreclosure.
   2. strict foreclosure.
   3. judicial foreclosure by sale.
   4. general foreclosure.

3. The Wisconsin usury law provides that the maximum interest rate, including points, that may be charged an individual on a real estate loan is

   1. 12 percent.
   2. 14 percent.
   3. 10 percent.
   4. unlimited.

4. In Wisconsin, the maximum veterans first-mortgage home loan is what percentage of the total cost?

   1. 90
   2. 70
   3. 95
   4. 100

5. In Wisconsin, mortgage agreements and land contracts may be made only

   1. where the interest is to be paid in monthly installments.
   2. where substantial sums of money are involved.
   3. on forms approved by the Wisconsin Department of Regulation and Licensing or the Wisconsin State Bar Association.
   4. during business hours.

6. Strict foreclosure is prohibited in Wisconsin

   1. when a land contract is involved.
   2. always.
   3. when the interest is more than 12 percent.
   4. when a mortgage is involved.

7. Which of the following statements does not correctly describe an aspect of a land contract?

   1. Buyers in a land contract sale should record the contract with the register of deeds.
   2. State Bar Form 10 is designated as the approved form in transactions that are not subject to the Wisconsin Consumer Act.
   3. A seller under a land contract may sue the defaulted borrower for judicial foreclosure.
   4. A land contract may be foreclosed by strict foreclosure.

8. Which of the following statements does not correctly describe the Wisconsin Consumer Act?

   1. The act may cover land contracts.
   2. The act may prevent the seller in a land contract from denying the buyer prepayment privileges.
   3. The act may not prohibit balloon payments.
   4. The act may undercut the seller's usual land contract remedies in case of default by limiting the use of acceleration clauses.

16

Leases

Leasehold Estates

Wisconsin recognizes four types of leasehold estates: *estate for years, periodic tenancy, tenancy at will* and *tenancy at sufferance.* Tenancy at sufferance is referred to as a holdover tenancy in Wisconsin. These are described in Chapter 16 of the text.

Statute of Frauds

The Wisconsin Statute of Frauds, as it applies to leases, requires that *all leases for more than a year be in writing.* A lease for one year or less may be made orally and still be valid.

Lease Forms

Forms for the lease of real property are no longer approved by the Wisconsin Department of Regulation and Licensing. Chapter RL16.04(2m) allows real estate licensees to use commercially available lease forms provided that the client approves of the forms. The rule states that a licensee may, when acting as an agent, use lease forms that have been drafted by the principal to the transaction or an attorney and have been approved by the licensee's client. The rule also states that the lease forms shall identify the drafter.

Chapter RL16.04(3m) states that a licensee may, when acting as a sole principal or one of several principals, use lease forms that have been drafted by the licensee or obtained from another source. Licensees were previously required to use lease forms drafted by an attorney where the licensee was either a tenant or a landlord.

Recording the Lease

A lease for more than one year is legally a conveyance under Chapter 706 of the Wisconsin Statutes. A lease, therefore, must meet the same requirements as a deed in order to be enforceable. A lease should be recorded to protect the interests of the parties involved and *to be valid against the claims of third parties without notice.* The lease must include all the terms and conditions of the agreement. It *must be signed by the parties, must identify the parties and must offer a reasonably definite description of the land. All material terms of the lease, the amount of rent and the commencement and expiration of the lease must be included.* The rights and duties of landlords and tenants are set forth in the Wisconsin Statutes.

Any special provisions not included in the statutes that are agreed on by both parties may be written into the lease. The general requirements of a valid lease are described in Chapter 16 of the text. *Wit-*

This material supplements Chapter 16 in *Modern Real Estate Practice* by Galaty, Allaway and Kyle.

nesses and acknowledgment are not essential to the validity of a lease in Wisconsin. A lease, however, must be acknowledged if it is to be recorded.

Termination of Leaseholds

An estate for years *terminates automatically at the end of the lease term* without advance notice from either the lessor or the lessee. A periodic tenancy and a tenancy at will may be terminated by giving at least *28 days' notice in writing* (Chapter 704.19). The Wisconsin Statutes require that the termination date set in the notice coincides with the end of the rent-paying period. The rules apply to both the lessor and lessee. In general, notice can be given more than 28 days in advance. An agreement between the lessor and lessee to terminate prior to the normal date or without statutory notice may be oral or written. However, if notice of termination is given more than one year before the normal date, it must be in writing. All tenancies may be terminated by mutual consent of the parties.

BREACH OF LEASE (CHAPTER 704)

Breach by Tenant

When a tenant fails to meet the terms specified and required in a lease, various remedies are available to the landlord. If, for example, a tenant remains in possession of the leased premises after the end of a tenancy without the landlord's consent, the landlord may either *collect double the amount of the daily rent for the number of days the tenant remains in possession or remove the tenant.* If a tenant vacates the premises before the end of the tenancy without paying the agreed-upon rent, the landlord may *recover the rent plus damages.* However, the landlord is required to minimize damages by making a reasonable effort to rent the premises after the tenant leaves.

If a month-to-month or week-to-week periodic tenant fails to pay rent, the landlord may give him or her a *5-day notice to pay or vacate or a 14-day notice to vacate.* If the tenant fails to pay within the 5-day pay-or-vacate period, the tenancy is terminated and the landlord may begin eviction proceedings. The tenant may not pay after the pay-or-vacate period has expired. Where the 14-day notice to vacate applies, the tenant cannot cure the default by paying rent.

Where a periodic tenant commits waste or breaches a lease *in any way other than nonpayment of rent,* the landlord may give a *14-day notice to vacate.* For a year-to-year tenant or a tenant under a lease for one year or less, the landlord may give a *5-day fix-or-vacate notice on the first violation of any lease term and a 14-day vacate notice on a second violation within a year.* For a tenant who has a lease for more than one year, the landlord may give a *30-day notice. A landlord is prohibited from terminating a tenant in retaliation for the tenant's reporting of housing code violations.*

Notice. A landlord may *deliver* notice personally or through the person in charge of the property, *send* notice by registered mail or another delivery service or *post* notice in a conspicuous place on the premises.

Breach by Landlord

When a landlord fails to furnish the specified services required in a lease, such as adequate heat, *the tenant may sue for damages.* Where the breach is serious enough to interfere with the tenant's enjoyment of the premises, the tenant may *move out and not be liable for further rent.* This provision applies only if the damages to the premises or the inconveniences suffered are caused by the landlord rather than by the tenant's own negligence.

In Wisconsin, a landlord may include an *exculpatory clause* in a lease, which provides that the landlord is *not liable for certain specified conditions,* which might include damage caused by bursting water pipes, floods or a leaky roof. This clause relieves the landlord of responsibility only for the specified conditions. Section AG134.08 places heavy restrictions on the use of an exculpatory clause in a lease.

Destruction of the Premises

If a property is destroyed or partially damaged by fire, the elements or any conditions hazardous to a tenant's health, and if the damage is not repaired immediately, the *tenant may vacate the premises and not be liable for rent.* If a tenant moves because of the hardship caused by the inconvenience of the repairs, *the tenant is not liable for the rent so long as the premises are unhabitable* or *untenable.* This provision applies only if the damage was not caused by the negligence of the tenant.

Automatic Extension Clauses

Automatic renewal or extension clauses in residential leases are *unenforceable* against a tenant unless the landlord *gives at least 15, but not more than 30, days' notice of this lease provision.*

Eviction

A landlord may institute eviction proceedings by serving and *filing summons* and *a written complaint* in the court of the county in which the premises are located. The sheriff of the county enforces any eviction rulings.

Types of Leases

The basic types of lease agreements—*gross leases, net leases and percentage leases*—are described in the text. A percentage-lease arrangement may be included as part of the terms of a gross or net lease.

Commercial and Farm Leases

Commercial and farm leases usually involve a contractual relationship extending over many years; therefore, they are much more complicated to prepare and negotiate than most leases. Farm leases vary substantially depending on what the lessor and lessee are furnishing to the farm operation besides land and labor and on what type of risk each party is willing to take. *Commercial leases* generally center on *flexible rental terms* to protect the lessor and lessee through the use of *percentage leases.* The lessor requires the lessee to provide adequate information that reflects sales and maximum utilization of the facilities. Payment of taxes and insurance is among the many considerations to be negotiated in a commercial lease. Commercial leases may contain tenant options for renewing the leases or for outright purchase, as well as for allowing for the leasing of a portion of a building, the balance of which may be retained by the landlord or leased to other tenants.

Residential Rental Practices Code

The Residential Rental Practices Code (AG134, Wis. Adm. Code) became effective on May 1, 1980. The code is the product of an extensive investigation into problems between landlords and tenants by the staff of the Department of Agriculture, Trade and Consumer Protection, performed at the request of the legislature.

The code is limited to problems that were documented during the department's investigation. It is intended to promote fair business practices in the rental of housing as well as to help ensure that landlords and tenants approach rental-agreement negotiations on equal terms so that informed rental-housing choices can be made.

AG134 does not, however, alter legal precedents or existing statutory law embodied in Chapter 704, Wisconsin Statutes, which is the basic law regulating landlord-tenant relations. Rather, it supplements and clarifies existing law in several respects, while at the same time addressing issues and business practices that are subject to Wisconsin's Unfair Trade Practices Act (S. 100.20, Wis. Stats.).

Included among the key provisions of the Residential Rental Practices Code are:

1.   When a security deposit is required, the code establishes specific elements of a mutual "check-in" procedure in order to objectively document preexisting damages. It requires landlords to provide tenants with a description of any physical damages charged against the previous tenant's security deposit. This description is to be provided before a security deposit is accepted or at the same time as notice to the previous tenant, whichever occurs later. The amount of the charges and the identity of the previous tenant need not be disclosed. If damages have been repaired, this can be noted in connection with the damage description. In addition, the tenant must be given no less than seven days in which to inspect and document other preexisting conditions.

2.   Security deposits, less any amounts withheld by the landlord, must be returned in person or by mail to the last known address of the tenant within 21 days after surrender of the premises.

3.   Where any deduction is made from the security deposit, the tenant must be provided with an itemized statement describing each item of damages or claim against the deposit and the amount withheld as reasonable compensation for each claim. A landlord is prohibited from intentionally falsifying any security deposit claim. For example, where a tenant's failure to clean certain portions of the premises is serious to the extent that it represents abuse, waste or neglect, the rule does not prohibit reasonable deductions from the security deposit as compensation for necessary cleaning at the conclusion of tenancy. However, routine across-the-board deductions for cleaning or carpet shampooing, unrelated to any abuse, waste or neglect by the tenant, are prohibited in the absence of a clear and separately negotiated written agreement, entered into at the time of initial rental.

The Wisconsin Department of Agriculture, Trade and Consumer Protection has published *Landlords and Tenants—The Wisconsin Way*. This publication provides the exact language of Chapter 704 (1977 edition, Wis. Stats.) and AG134. It also contains an extensive explanation of the provisions of AG134 and how it complements existing law.

Copies of this publication are available from:

Wisconsin Department of Agriculture, Trade and Consumer Protection
801 West Badger Road, P.O. Box 8911
Madison, WI 53708
Phone: Madison area—(608) 266-7228, Milwaukee area—(414) 342-3020
Toll-free number—1-800-362-3020

One copy may be obtained free of charge; additional copies are available at $.50 per copy.

QUESTIONS

1. Which of the following statements does not correctly describe a specific lease?

    1. A lease for more than one year is legally a conveyance.
    2. A lease should be recorded to protect the interests of the parties involved.
    3. Wisconsin licensees must use a department-approved form for an apartment lease.
    4. A lease for one year or less may be made orally and still be enforceable.

2. If a week-to-week periodic tenant fails to pay rent, the landlord may give him or her a

    1. 5-day notice to pay or vacate.
    2. 10-day notice to pay or vacate.
    3. 15-day notice to pay or vacate.
    4. 20-day notice to pay or vacate.

3. A tenant has a month-to-month tenancy in an apartment building. The tenant failed to pay the rent for the month of June and the landlord has given him a 14-day notice to vacate. The tenant

    1. may pay the rent and continue to live in the apartment building.
    2. must vacate immediately after the 14 days are up.
    3. may take the landlord to court.
    4. may ignore the notice to vacate.

4. Which of the following statements does not correctly describe the Residential Rental Practices Code?

    1. The code is AG134 Wisconsin Administrative Code.
    2. The code is intended to promote fair business practices in the rental of housing.
    3. The code alters legal precedents embodied in Chapter 704, Wisconsin Statutes.
    4. The code clarifies existing law.

5. You are renting an apartment from a landlord who requires a security deposit. As part of the check-in procedure, the landlord is required to provide you with

    1. a description of any physical damages charged against the previous tenant's security deposit.
    2. the amount of damages charged against the previous tenant's security deposit.
    3. the name of the previous tenant.
    4. no less than three days in which to inspect and document preexisting conditions.

6. Security deposits, less any amounts withheld by a landlord, must be returned in person or by mail to the last known address of the tenant within how many days after surrender of the premises?

    1. 7
    2. 14
    3. 21
    4. 28

7. Which of the following statements does not correctly describe the current status of forms for the lease of real property in Wisconsin?

    1. Real estate licensees may use commercially available lease forms, provided that the client approves of the forms.
    2. Real estate licensees must use lease forms approved by the Wisconsin Department of Regulation and Licensing.
    3. A real estate licensee acting as a principal may use forms that have been drafted by the licensee.
    4. Forms for the lease of real property are no longer approved by the Wisconsin Department of Regulation and Licensing.

Control of Land Use and Property Development and Subdivision

Plan Commission and Zoning Board of Adjustment

Land use in Wisconsin is planned and controlled by *local plan commissions* and *other local public agencies* in cities, towns and villages. These plan commissions deal with the preparation of the master plan for an area. They *hold hearings* and are involved in the preparation of *zoning ordinances* and *zoning amendments*. There are no such plan commissions in Wisconsin counties. County planning functions are carried out by either the *county park commission* or a *zoning committee of the county board.*

In Wisconsin cities, the plan commission consists of seven members, including the mayor, the city engineer, the president of the park board, an alderperson and three citizens. The *zoning board of adjustment* is common to both city and rural zoning. The board of adjustment *hears appeals from actions of the building inspector or other zoning administrators and has powers to grant use variances.* The board may, under a particular zoning ordinance, *grant special-use permits* for exceptional uses.

Zoning

All Wisconsin towns (under certain conditions), counties, villages and cities have zoning powers. In addition, villages and fourth-class cities have power to zone one and one-half miles beyond their corporate limits. *Larger cities can exercise extraterritorial power up to three miles outside their limits.* This power can be exercised only if a specific procedure is followed: The town board for the outlying area must appoint three persons to join the three citizen members of the village or city plan commission. If the majority of the six approve extraterritorial zoning, they can recommend that it be adopted by the village or city governing board.

Subdivision Regulations

Wisconsin's Subdivision Code is covered in Chapter 236 of the Wisconsin Statutes. All land in the state is subject to the Code. However, the state regulations govern only *where five or more lots of one and one-half acres or less in area are created within a period of five years for the purpose of sale or building development.* Chapter 236 does not apply where the parcels are larger than one and one-half acres or where four lots or fewer are created. Local units of government, however, are authorized to adopt more stringent regulations and certain municipalities have done so. In those cases where more stringent controls have not been adopted, Section 236.34 permits the use of a *certified survey map for four or fewer parcels* to provide greater accuracy in real estate descriptions.

Subdivision plats. *Copies of all subdivision plats must be sent to the director of local and regional planning of the Wisconsin Department of Development for review.* In a case where the land borders on a

---

This material supplements Chapters 19 and 20 in *Modern Real Estate Practice* by Galaty, Allaway and Kyle.

state trunk highway, the director submits copies of the plat to the Department of Transportation for review. The director also sends copies to the Department of Health for review where the subdivision is not to be served by a public sewer. The county also may review the plat and, if the land is located in an unincorporated town, the plat also must be reviewed by the town board. *The final plat will not be accepted for the public records by the register of deeds until all of these public bodies are satisfied with the plat.* Any subdivider or agent who offers subdivided land for sale knowing that the final plat has not been recorded is subject to a fine of $500 or imprisonment for up to six months or both.

Out-of-State Unimproved Properties or Subdivision Lots

Effective February 1, 1982, Chapter REB 5 of the Wisconsin Administrative Code was repealed by the Wisconsin Real Estate Examining Board. The former rule required that brokers and developers (indirectly) make certain arrangements pertaining to the release of individual lots from encumbrances and for the complete and full information to purchasers concerning the seller's interest in the land and concerning the existence of any encumbrances. This rule required that documents be filed with the Real Estate Examining Board showing that such arrangements had been made. At present, no filing of any kind must be made with the new Real Estate Board or the Department of Regulation and Licensing for marketing out-of-state subdivision lots. Any person who physically markets such lots in Wisconsin, even owners who are involved in a pattern of sales of their own properties, must have a Wisconsin real estate license or utilize the services of a Wisconsin licensee. Such licensees must observe all usual statutory and rule requirements and especially pay attention to requirements relating to full disclosure, approved contractual forms and real estate trust funds.

Shoreland Zoning

The Wisconsin shoreland zoning laws were adopted in 1966. Their objectives include

1.   furthering the maintenance of healthful conditions;

2.   preventing and controlling water pollution;

3.   protecting spawning grounds, fish and aquatic life;

4.   controlling building sites, placement of structures and land uses; and

5.   preserving shore cover and natural beauty.

The 1966 laws require zoning of all land in unincorporated areas (outside city or village limits) within *1,000 feet of a lake, pond or flowage and all land within 300 feet of a river or stream or to the landward side of a floodplain,* whichever distance is greater. The law provides that county ordinance implement shoreland zoning, but if the county fails to adopt an ordinance that meets reasonable minimum standards, the *Wisconsin Department of Natural Resources (DNR)* may adopt a zoning ordinance that applies to the county. However, if a town has a zoning ordinance that is more restrictive than that adopted by the county, *the more restrictive provisions remain in effect.*

In Wisconsin, shoreland areas are subject to zoning regulations that include

1.   minimum standards for water supply and waste disposal;

2.   tree-cutting regulations;

3.   setbacks for structures from highways and navigable waters;

4.   minimum lot sizes;

5.   grading controls;

6.   lagooning and dredging regulations; and

7.   subdivision regulations.

Farmland Preservation Act (Section 91 of the Wisconsin Statutes)

The Farmland Preservation Act *provides an income tax credit to Wisconsin residents who own at least 35 acres of farmland in Wisconsin.* The farmland must either *be zoned for exclusive agricultural use or be subject to a farmland-preservation agreement.* In addition, the farmland must have produced at least $6,000 in gross farm profits during the year preceding application for a farmland-preservation agreement or a total of at least $18,000 of gross farm profits during the three years preceding application. A farmland-preservation agreement refers to a restrictive covenant, evidenced by an instrument, whereby the owner and the state agree to hold jointly *the right to develop the land* except as may be expressly reserved in the instrument. Such an agreement also may contain a covenant running with the land for a term of years *not to develop* except as expressly reserved in the instrument.

Floodplain Zoning (Section 87 of the Wisconsin Statutes)

All floodplains in Wisconsin are now or soon will be subject to zoning. The Wisconsin Department of Natural Resources will adopt zoning for any floodplain for which a county, city or village does not adopt zoning. The basic purposes of floodplain regulations are to

1.   protect, life, health and property;

2.   minimize expenditures of public monies for costly flood-control projects;

3.   minimize rescue and relief efforts generally undertaken at the expense of the general public;

4.   minimize business interruptions;

5.   minimize damage to public facilities on the floodplains, such as water mains, sewer lines, streets and bridges;

6.   minimize the occurrence of future flood-blight areas on floodplains; and

7.   discourage the victimization of unwary land and home buyers.

The 1981 Wisconsin Legislature created Sections 61.351 and 65.231 of the statutes, requiring villages and cities to zone by ordinance all unfilled wetlands of five acres or more that are shown on the final wetland inventory maps prepared by the Department of Natural Resources for the village or city that are located in any shorelands and within its incorporated area at any time.

Any citizen of the state may bring action in court to force the removal of any structure, fill or development placed in a floodplain in violation of any ordinance, and the one who placed it there may be fined up to $50 per day until it is removed. For more information, see Chapter NR, Wisconsin Administrative Code.

Building Code

A new state Uniform Building Code for single-family homes and duplexes went into effect June 1, 1980. It sets minimum standards for structure, heating, ventilation and fire safety of conventional and manufactured housing. The new code specifies everything from the types of fasteners to be used in home building to mandatory installation of smoke detectors. The code allows for innovative building techniques by specifying how a building ultimately must perform, rather than exactly how it must be built.

In Wisconsin, the *Homeowners' Warranty* (HOW) *Program* is provided for those who are concerned about home-building problems. Building firms enrolled in the HOW program can *insure homeowners against major defects in the homes that they build.*

The HOW program began in 1973 and includes a *ten-year warranty* against major structural defects. Faulty workmanship and defective materials are covered for the first year, and the builder guarantees plumbing, heating, electricity and cooling systems for the first two years. Builder guarantees are underwritten by mutual insurance coverage. The builder pays up to $5 for each $1,000 of the cost of the home to participate in the program. The program for the Milwaukee, Madison, Racine and Kenosha areas is handled through the HOW Council of Greater Milwaukee. The Wisconsin Builders Association handles the program for the rest of the state.

Wisconsin Environmental Policy Act

The Wisconsin Environmental Policy Act (WEPA—Chapters 273 and 274 of the Wisconsin Statutes) became effective in April 1972. It is patterned after the National Environmental Policy Act, which became effective in January 1970. *WEPA requires each state agency to prepare a detailed statement concerning the environmental effects of any proposed action that could significantly affect the quality of the environment* and to obtain the comments of any other agency that may have jurisdiction or special expertise with respect to the environmental impact of the proposed action. When a course of action involves unresolved conflicts in the use of resources, WEPA requires state agencies to study, develop and describe appropriate alternatives. *State agencies also are required to initiate and utilize ecological information in the planning and development of resource-oriented projects.*

In Wisconsin, real estate licensees who engage in land development also are subject to environmental controls. Chapter 273 of the Wisconsin Statutes gives the Wisconsin Department of Natural Resources the power to grant permits to develop land on statutory approval. The DNR may require developers to submit *environmental impact statements if the area to be developed is more than 40 acres or if the cost of the project exceeds $25,000.*

QUESTIONS

1. Larger cities in Wisconsin have been given power to zone how many miles beyond their corporate limits?

   1. One and one-half
   2. Two
   3. Three
   4. Five

2. Which of the following statements does not correctly describe the zoning board of adjustment?

   1. The board may have the power to grant special-use permits.
   2. The board is common to both city and rural zonings.
   3. The board hears appeals from actions of the building inspector.
   4. The board may change the zoning on a parcel of land.

3. In Wisconsin cities, the plan commission consists of how many members, including the mayor?

    1. Seven   3. Five
    2. Six   4. Four

4. Copies of all subdivision plats must be sent for review to the

    1. director of the Department of Regulation and Licensing.
    2. director of local and regional planning.
    3. director of the Department of Labor, Industry and Human Relations.
    4. executive secretary of the Real Estate Board.

5. Which of the following statements is *not* an objective of Wisconsin shoreland zoning law?

    1. Furthering the maintenance of healthful conditions
    2. Minimizing business interruptions
    3. Preventing and controlling water pollution
    4. Preserving shore cover and natural beauty

6. Which of the following statements is true of a farmland-preservation agreement?

    1. It provides an income tax credit to anyone who owns farmland in Wisconsin.
    2. It provides an income tax credit to anyone who owns at least 35 acres of farmland in Wisconsin.
    3. It requires that farmland be zoned for conservation.
    4. It may contain a covenant for a term of years not to develop land except as expressly reserved in the agreement.

23

Closing the Real Estate Transaction

In Wisconsin, most real estate transactions are closed *in the office of the lending institution* that is financing the sale or *in the office of a title insurance company.* In those cases where no lending institution or title insurance company is involved, closings generally are held at an *attorney's office* or at the *office of the real estate broker.* The seller's attorney is responsible for all details of the transaction that concern the title to the property, such as preparing the deed and making sure that any prior liens have been repaid. The buyer's attorney makes the necessary disbursements of the buyer's checks.

Broker's Role at the Closing

It is usually the broker's responsibility to ensure that the parties appear at the designated time and place with the appropriate documents and that arrangements have been made for any special factors, such as a measurement of the seller's existing supply of heating fuel. *The seller's broker usually prepares the closing statement and collects his or her commission at the closing.* The broker also should make sure that copies of the closing statement are made for each of the sellers, the buyers and their attorneys. The broker may delegate the preparation of the closing statement to almost anyone, but the broker remains ultimately responsible.

Evidence of Title

In Wisconsin, *the seller is required to furnish* and pay for satisfactory evidence of title in the form of either an *abstract or title insurance; title insurance is generally being used in most real estate transactions.* The *buyer is responsible for examining the title* to the real estate that is being purchased. The buyer generally has his or her own attorney examine the title and pays the attorney's fees. However, increasingly less reliance is being placed on title searches made by attorneys. As discussed in Chapter 12 of this supplement, most lenders are requiring the buyer to obtain a *title insurance commitment* as of the date of sale to protect their interests. In addition to this *mortgage title insurance policy,* the buyer's attorney usually will recommend that the buyer purchase an *owner's title insurance policy* to protect the buyer's interest as well. The title insurance company's decision to issue a policy generally is based on an abstract of title, prepared for this purchase by a professional abstractor.

As additional protection, most lenders also will require buyers to have a licensed surveyor prepare a *survey* of the real estate being purchased.

CLOSING PROBLEM

The following problem uses the procedures involved in an actual real estate transaction in Wisconsin. The data given in this problem have been used to complete the listing contract reproduced in Chapter

This material supplements Chapter 23 in *Modern Real Estate Practice* by Galaty, Allaway and Kyle.

5 of this supplement, as well as the offer to purchase that appears in Chapter 10. The student is advised to study these examples after reading the closing problem.

Data Describing the Real Estate Transaction

John James, a salesperson for Newhouse Realty, which is a member of the local REALTORS®
Multiple-Listing Service, secured a four-month exclusive listing on September 13, 1994, from
George and Martha Carter. The listing was for their home at 1400 Regas Lane, Madison, Wisconsin
53705. The legal description is Lot 2, Block 4, of the Fairmont Subdivision, NW½ of Section 8, T9N,
R7E, Dane County, Wisconsin. The Carters agreed to include the refrigerator, washer, dryer, carpeting, drapes and drapery rods in the total selling price of $56,900. The Carters will give occupancy on
the date of closing. James has agreed to hold at least one open house and to list the property with a
multiple-listing service.

First Federal Bank of Madison holds a mortgage on the Carters' property with an unpaid balance of
$26,650 as of September 1. The monthly payment, including interest, is $275.10; interest is charged
at the rate of 8 percent per annum; and the final payment is to be made within 13 years. The bank has
indicated that this mortgage may be assumed by a qualified buyer at the same rate of interest.

On November 15, 1994, salesperson James obtained an offer from Jay and Linda Jones to purchase
the property for $56,000. The offer was made on the basis of the buyers' assumption of the balance
of the existing mortgage and the balance of the selling price being paid in cash at closing. Possession
was desired as of the date of closing, which was to be no later than December 15, 1994. If the Carters
occupy the property after the closing, they agree to pay $25 per day for each day they remain on the
property. The Joneses paid earnest money of $2,000, with another $2,000 to be paid on acceptance of
the offer. The offer was accepted by the Carters on November 16. 1994.

Real estate taxes for 1994 have not been paid yet. They must be prorated and credited to the buyers,
who will actually pay the taxes when they become due. Taxes for 1994 were $1,224. The buyers will
assume the Carters' home insurance policy from Celtic Insurance Company, which runs from May 1,
1994, to April 30, 1995, at a cost of $390. James paid $318.50 for an owner's title insurance policy
on behalf of the Carters; he also paid the transfer tax appropriate for the transaction. The Carters
agree to pay an attorney's fee of $100 for preparation of the deed.

James has made arrangements for the sellers' water, gas and electric meters to be read on the day of
closing and billed accordingly on the closing statement. The water bill is $20 and the combined gas
and electric bill is $80. The broker's commission, as agreed to in the listing contract, is 7 percent of
the selling price.

The buyers in this transaction are responsible for the $2 recording fee charged for filing the deed.
They agree to pay the lender a 1 percent assumption fee on the remaining balance of the loan and to
reimburse the lender for the $15 credit report. The buyers also need a title insurance mortgage policy,
which costs $18. Their attorney's fee is $100. The buyers' expenses are not figured on the closing
statement.

Completing the Closing Statement

Complete the blank closing statement at the back of this chapter using the data in the preceding problem. Prorate all expenses using the actual number of days in a month and 365 days in a year. Carry all computations to three decimal places and then round off. **Do not** round off to two places until the final answer is found. The Wisconsin closing statement form used in this supplement is similar to the single statement form used in the text. After completing the closing statement, check your answers against the form in the Answer Key. An explanation of the closing statement follows this section.

Computing the prorations and charges. Following are illustrations of the various steps in computing the prorations and other amounts included in the closing statement.

1.   Closing date: December 15, 1994

2.   Commission: 7 percent × $56,000 (sales price) = $3,920

3.   Assumed mortgage principal and interest: The unpaid balance of the sellers' mortgage was $26,650 as of September 1 (the listing was taken September 13, 1994). Because the sale was closed on December 15, three more monthly payments were made by the sellers and the balance reduced as follows:

Date	Balance
September 1	$26,650.00
October 1	$26,550.13
November 1	$26,455.42
December 1	$26,354.27

Therefore, the unpaid balance of the assumed mortgage on December 15 was the December 1 balance, and the prorated interest is based on that figure. The interest proration is for December 1 to 15:

$26,354.27 × 8% = $2,108.3416 per year
$2,108.3416 ÷ 365 days in a year = 5.7762
15 days of earned interest to be paid by sellers
14 × $5.7762 = *$80.87 interest owed by sellers*

Because the buyers agree to assume the sellers' remaining mortgage debt, the balance of the principal remaining is credited to them, as is the interest that accrued on that principal while the sellers had possession of the property during part of December.

4.   Insurance: The insurance premium has been paid in advance by the sellers. The buyers will reimburse them for the unearned portion.

$50,000 policy, three-year premium for $390, expires April 30, 1996
$390 ÷ 3 = $130 (yearly premium)
$130 ÷ 365 = $.3562 (daily rate)

Total number of days covered beyond December 15, 1994 = 501

1 year	365 days
December 16–31	15 days
January	31 days
February	28 days
March	31 days
April	30 days
	500 days

500 × $.3562 (daily rate) = *$178.10 due sellers*

5. Estimated real estate taxes for 1994: $1,224 (estimate based on 1993 tax)

$1,224 ÷ 365 days = $3.353 per day
Earned period from January 1, 1994, to and including December 14, 1994 = 348 days
348 ÷ 365 = .9534

.953 × $1,224 = $1,166.47 = *$1,166.47 credit to buyers*

SAMPLE CLOSING STATEMENTS AND EXPLANATION

The sample buyer's and seller's closing statements found at the end of this chapter (see Figures 23.1 and 23.2) are based on the sale of a home as follows:

Buyer's Closing Statement

The agreed-on sales price was $56,000 and the buyer made an earnest-money payment of $4,000. These are shown on lines 1 and 2 of the form.

The property was sold to the buyers subject to a mortgage that the buyers assumed and agreed to pay. The unpaid balance as of the date of closing is shown as a credit on line 4.

You should write the local treasurer's office and ask it to check for any delinquent property taxes. You should also ask for a breakdown of the tax bills paid for the prior year. The treasurer's office also will tell you if there are any deferred taxes. All replies should be in writing. If you find delinquent taxes, you should request a letter showing the interest due. Any delinquent tax paid on or after the first of any month will include an interest charge for the entire month.

Line 5 would be used only if the buyers were buying the property subject to a mortgage and the mortgage holder had been collecting money regularly from the sellers in order to pay the taxes or insurance premiums when they came due. Any of the sellers' money in the possession of the mortgage holder would be shown as "due seller" on line 5.

Taxes were not delinquent in the sample problem. If the taxes had been delinquent and if the buyers had assumed and agreed to pay them, the amount of delinquent taxes as of the date of closing would be shown as a credit to the buyers on line 6.

Prior to the closing, you should check the parcel number and assessed value with either the assessor or the clerk in your municipality. You can check the current year's taxes with the local treasurer's office. If these offices do not have the information, they will direct you to the proper source. For most of the year, when no recent new improvements have been added, taxes are prorated on the basis of the net general tax for the previous year; however, later in the year, you should take into account possible higher current-year assessed values and mill-rate changes as known.

The expected taxes for the year 1994 were prorated through the day *prior to closing* based on the amount of tax for 1994 and a calendar year of 365 days. Taxes in 1993 were $1,224. The sellers owned the property 348 days in 1994 and are paying that proportionate part of the year's taxes. This is shown as a credit to the buyers on line 7.

When writing to the local treasurer's office, you should also ask it to check for unpaid special assessments and future special assessments. Be careful that you know what they are for and the exact amount, if available, it will take to pay them in full. It is a good policy, especially where recent special assessments are suspected, to check with the engineering department or the clerk's office in your municipality to get its preliminary figures for any such work being done. These figures can be used as a basis of an escrow pending completion of the work and determination of the actual cost. Sidewalk repairs and tree removal are common special assessments on older properties, while sewer, water and street curb and gutter are common in newer areas.

There were no special assessments against the property. If there were unpaid special assessments that under the purchase agreement were to be paid by the sellers, and if they were assumed by the buyers as of the date of closing, they would be shown as a credit to the buyers on line 8. This approach can provide additional financing for a buyer. Assume that a property has a special assessment against it for $500 payable in five yearly installments. By assuming the special assessment that the seller would otherwise have to pay, the buyer is immediately credited with the payment of $500 on the purchase price, but the buyer actually will have five years in which to pay the money. The buyer will have to pay interest to the municipality, but often it will be at no higher rate than the buyer is paying on other borrowed money.

There is no tenant in the house. Therefore, you do not have to account for rental income. In the case of rented property, written approval of the tenants should be obtained prior to transferring security deposits on the closing statement. In addition, rents should be prorated between the parties. If the closing is taking place prior to the next rent-paying date, the buyer, of course, will collect the rent for the next rental period. If the closing is on or after the rent-paying date, the seller should collect the rent and give the buyer credit on the statement. Let's suppose for illustrative purposes that there is a tenant in another house who will not be moving until May 30. The tenant is paying rent at the rate of $100 per month in advance. The tenant pays the seller the April rent on April 1; the house is purchased on April 15. The rent for the last half of the month belongs to the buyer, so he or she would be credited with $50 on line 9. The buyers and the sellers estimated that the fuel oil tank contained about 100 gallons worth $80. This is shown on line 10. It is best to arrange with the seller to have the tank filled and charge the purchaser for a full tank on the closing statement. However, if the seller is opposed to having the tank filled, it may be prorated. You should call the oil company to determine the tank capacity, type of oil used and cost per gallon. You should then have the gauge on the tank read to determine the amount in the tank and to compute the credit due the seller. Some oil companies will read the tank and calculate this for you. You should check with the buyer before you ask the seller to fill the tank.

In some cases, additional instruments have to be recorded to show clear title in the seller before the buyer will accept his or her deed. The cost of recording instruments for this purpose is the responsibility of the seller. As a matter of convenience, occasionally, the instruments are recorded by the buyer. When this happens, the buyer is credited for the recording fees on line 11.

If a land contract is being recorded, the Wisconsin Real Estate Transfer Return form must be completed by the vendor for submission at the time the contract is recorded; the Wisconsin transfer fee is paid at that time. It must be signed by both the buyer and the seller, setting forth the value of the ownership interest transferred by the land contract. When the contract has been paid off, the deed is offered for recording. Because the fee is imposed by law on the seller, but in practice the deed will be recorded by the buyer or the buyer's attorney and the fee paid by the buyer, the buyer will receive credit for the amount of the fee on the closing.

The buyer, as he or she records the land contract, will have to pay the Wisconsin transfer fee, which by statute is the responsibility of the seller. The buyer is credited with this amount on line 12. Thus, the transfer fee of $168 (30 cents per $100 of the value of the property) is shown as a credit to the buyers on line 12. However, in this case, the broker paid the transfer fee, which will be noted later.

When an insurance policy is being assigned, you should contact the agent for the company name, policy number, type of coverage, amount of coverage, term of policy and amount of premium and what premium has been paid.

The buyers are assuming the sellers' fire insurance policy. Therefore, the purchase agreement provides for proration of insurance. The sellers have a three-year fire insurance policy that is $390 and that would not expire until April 30, 1996. The buyers are receiving 501 days of insurance coverage for which they must pay $178.10. This amount is shown on line 13 as being due the seller.

The totals show that the sellers are entitled to a total payment of $56,258.10 for the property and fuel oil, and that the buyers have received credit for $31,601.61 of that amount. The buyers still owe $24,656.49, which they must pay before they receive the deed.

The balance due the sellers (lines 16 through 20) will be made up of a check for or cash of $24,656.49 on line 18, for the total of $24,656.49 on line 20. The seller's closing statement showing the broker's settlement with the sellers is completed as follows.

Seller's Closing Statement

This form shows the amount that a broker has received for a seller (a buyer's down payment), the balance due from the buyer and the deductions of the amounts that are owed by the seller to the broker. It also shows the net balance due the seller.

In the sample problem, the cash balance due from the buyers to the sellers at the closing is shown as due the sellers on line 1. It is $24,656.49.

The buyers' down payment of $4,000, which has been held by the broker in his trust account, is shown on line 2.

Often as a matter of convenience for the seller, the broker as agent orders and is billed for and pays the cost of the abstract extension or title insurance that shows the title in the seller's name. This is an expense that is the responsibility of the seller. The $318.50 charge for providing the owner's title insurance policy is shown as a charge to the sellers on line 4.

Let's assume that title examination by the buyers' attorney discloses defects in the title and three instruments were recorded to show clear title in the sellers before giving the deed to the buyers. For the convenience of the sellers, the broker recorded them, but the payment of the recording fees is the responsibility of the sellers. The sellers are charged this cost of $10 on line 5.

The broker paid the transfer fee for the seller. The $168 transfer fee is shown as a charge on line 6.

The broker, with proper authority, has paid attorney fees for which the sellers were responsible. The $90 fee is shown as a charge on line 7.

Any advances that the broker has properly made for the sellers and any payments to be made for the sellers at the closing, such as the balance of the existing mortgage due or delinquent taxes, are charged to the sellers on lines 8–11.

Line 12 could be used for an occupancy escrow if called for by the contract; however, in this problem, occupancy was given to the buyers on the date of closing.

The broker's commission (7 percent times the $56,000 sales price) is charged to the sellers on line 13.

Any extra services performed by the broker for which he or she can properly make additional charges are shown on lines 14–16. The broker has made arrangements for the sellers' water, gas and electric meters to be read on the day of the closing. The sellers agree to escrow money with the broker to cover these expenses. The water bill escrow is $20. The combined gas and electric bill escrow is $80,

Figure 23.1   Buyer's Closing Statement

Form 930-B Rev. 4/86	**Nelco Forms** P.O. Box 10208 Green Bay, WI 54307-0208 414-337-1000

Buyer's Closing Statement

Broker

Property Location _____

Seller(s)
(Name and address) _____

Buyer(s)
(Name and address) _____

Contract date _____   Closing date _____   Closed at _____

BUYER'S SETTLEMENT WITH BROKER	Due Seller	Credit Buyer
1. Sale price	$	
2. Earnest money paid by Buyer		$
3. Downpayment by Buyer (in addition to Earnest money)...............................		
4. Mortgages or land contracts assumed by Buyer:_____		
5. Trust funds due Seller held by mortgagee:_____		
*6. Delinquent taxes assumed for years _____		
*7. Seller's share of taxes for _____ prorated from _____ to _____, prorated on a _____ basis @ $ _____ per _____, to be paid by Buyer (Last Year's taxes were $ _____).....................		
*8. Future installments of special assessment assumed by Buyer		
9. Rent prorated (see below)......................................		
10. Fuel oil and other items on premises:_____		
*11. Recording fees		
*12. Real estate transfer fees		
13. _____		
14. _____		
15. _____		
16. **TOTALS**..	$	$
17. Credits to Buyer (Enter total of second column on line 16)		
18. Balance due from Buyer (Line 16 less line 17).......................................	$	
19. Less: Mortgage or land contract executed by Buyer to Seller		
Other: _____		
20. Check or cash from Buyer to Broker (Line 18 less line 19)	$	

TENANT'S NAME	MONTHLY RENTAL	PAYABLE	DATE PAID UP TO	PRORATED AMOUNT

*This item could appear on the closing statement between the Broker and Seller but not on both.

Use and Occupancy - Broker will escrow $ _____ for use and occupancy charge and $ _____ to guarantee delivery of possession to Buyer until the property is vacated by the Seller, which includes the day of vacating. Any balance of the escrow money will be returned to the Seller upon vacating and delivery of keys to Broker.

Daily use and occupancy charge is $ _____. Date of vacating this property will be _____
Other - Seller certifies that he will leave all non-real estate items on the premises as agreed upon in the purchase agreement. Seller shall have all meters read prior to vacating and agrees to pay any delinquent or outstanding bills promptly upon receipt of such bill.

THIS STATEMENT IS ACCEPTED AS CORRECT _____ , 19 _____

_____ Buyer   _____ Seller

_____ Buyer   _____ Seller

930B NTF 0056B

Form provided by Nelco Inc. Used by permission.

Figure 23.2   Seller's Closing Statement

Form 930-S
Rev. 4 86

Nelco Forms
P.O. Box 10208
Green Bay, WI 54307-0208
414-337-1000

Seller's Closing Statement

Broker

Property Location _____

Seller(s)
(Name and address) _____

Buyer(s)
(Name and address) _____

Contract date _____   Closing date _____   Closed at _____

BROKER'S SETTLEMENT WITH SELLER	Charges against Seller	Due Seller
1. Check or cash received from Buyer (line 20 of Form 930-B)		$
2. Earnest money and down payment received from Buyer		
3. Total Amount Due Seller before charges against Seller (Line 1 plus line 2)		$
4. Abstract extention or title policy _____	$	
*5. Recording fees _____		
*6. Real estate transfer fee		
7. Attorney fees paid to _____		
8. Mortgage or land contract paid by Broker _____		
*9. Delinquent taxes paid by Broker for years _____		
*10. Seller's share of taxes for _____ prorated from _____ to _____ , prorated on a _____ basis @ $ _____ per _____ , to be paid by Broker (Last Year's taxes were $ _____)		
*11. Special assessments paid by Broker _____		
12. Other advances by Broker _____		
13. Commission		
14. Services by Broker (Itemize) _____		
15. _____		
16. _____		
17. _____		
18. _____		
19. _____		
20. _____		
21. **TOTAL Charges Against Seller**		$
22. Balance Due Seller (Line 3 less line 21)		$

*This item could appear on the closing statment between the Buyer and Broker but not on both.

Use and Occupancy - Broker will escrow $ _____ for use and occupancy charge and $ _____ to guarantee delivery of possession to Buyer until the property is vacated by the Seller, which includes the day of vacating. Any balance of the escrow money will be returned to the Seller upon vacating and delivery of keys to Broker.

Daily use and occupancy charge is $ _____ . Date of vacating this property will be _____

Other - Seller certifies that he will leave all non-real estate items on the premises as agreed upon in the purchase agreement. Seller shall have all meters read prior to vacating and agrees to pay any delinquent or outstanding bills promptly upon receipt of such bill.

THIS STATEMENT IS ACCEPTED AS CORRECT _____ , 19 _____

_____ Broker   _____ Seller

By _____   _____ Seller

930S NTF 0057C

which will be billed to the seller rather than paid for at the closing. The water bill charge is shown on lines 15 and 16.

The "total charges against seller" are $4,526.50 and the net balance of $24,129.99 is due the sellers.

The broker, on receipt of the water bill and gas and electric bills, will make the disbursement from the trust account for these expenses out of the funds escrowed. Any unused escrow funds would be returned to the sellers, as specified in an escrow agreement prepared in accordance with RL18.07.

The bottom of Form 930 shows the prorations. Prorate all expenses using the actual number of days in a month and 365 days in a year. Carry all computations to three decimal places and then round off. Do not round off to two places until the final answer is found. The Wisconsin closing statement form used in this supplement is similar to the single statement form used in the text. After completing the closing statement, check your answers against the forms in the Answer Key.

QUESTIONS

1. At the closing, the seller's broker usually does not

   1. ensure that the parties appear at the designated time and place.
   2. prepare the closing statement.
   3. collect his or her commission.
   4. prepare the deed.

2. In the closing statement for a real estate transaction, the earnest money deposit is charged as a

   1. credit to the seller.
   2. credit to the buyer.
   3. charge due the buyer.
   4. charge due the seller.

3. In order to protect their interests, many lenders in Wisconsin require a borrower to

   1. have a survey made on the real estate involved.
   2. obtain an owner's title insurance policy.
   3. obtain a title insurance commitment as of the date of sale.
   4. Both *1* and *3*

4. The person responsible for furnishing and paying for satisfactory title evidence in Wisconsin real estate transactions is the

   1. seller's attorney.
   2. seller.
   3. buyer.
   4. buyer's broker.

Use your completed closing statements for the closing problem on pages 94 and 95 to answer questions 5 through 9.

5. The amount due from the buyers at the closing is

   1. $31,612.76.
   2. $24,656.59.
   3. $ 4,494.50.
   4. $24,071.20.

6. The unpaid principal of the assumed mortgage is

   1. $26,650.00.
   2. $26,600.60.
   3. $26,355.76.
   4. $26,354.27.

7. At the closing, the sellers will receive

   1. $28,565.70.
   2. $24,129.99.
   3. $24,565.70.
   4. $31,612.76.

8. The sellers' expenses in the transaction include

   1. a title insurance policy.
   2. prorated insurance.
   3. special assessment taxes.
   4. prorated rents.

9. The broker's commission in this transaction is

   1. based on 7 percent of the list price.
   2. $3,360
   3. $3,920
   4. $4,480

10. Real estate taxes are prorated through the

    1. day prior to closing.
    2. day of closing.
    3. day after closing.
    4. second day after closing.

Special Lesson

Real Estate License Examination

Modern Real Estate Practice and the *Wisconsin Supplement* are designed to prepare you for a career in real estate. But before opening a brokerage office or a salesperson's listing book, you have to obtain a license, for which you must pass an examination, a test of what you have learned about real estate laws, principles and practices.

Why is a prelicensing examination important? A test is a measure of your ability to do something or your knowledge of a particular subject. The Wisconsin Department of Regulation and Licensing requires each license applicant to take an exam, not arbitrarily to keep people out of the real estate business, but to keep those people out of the industry who are not competent enough to practice real estate sales and brokerage.

Real estate licensing exams vary throughout the country in form and content. They utilize every form of question, from multiple-choice and true-false to essay questions and math problems. But whatever test form is used, each examination reflects the attitudes of the state's real estate licensing agency by stressing the areas of real estate knowledge that its members feel are important.

The Wisconsin real estate licensing examination is now administered and prepared by an independent testing service, the Psychological Services Inc. (PSI) program. A number of states subscribe to the PSI program. In each state, the program is adapted to local real estate laws and practices and the individual priorities of the state's licensing agency.

Wisconsin examinees are now taking the exam by computer. Taking the PSI examination by computer is simple; neither computer experience not typing skills are required for taking the test that will require you to use fewer than 12 keys. Upon being seated at the computer terminal, you will be prompted to confirm your name, identification number and the examination for which you are registered.

An introduction to the computer and keyboard will appear on the screen prior to your starting the exam. The time allowed for this introduction will not count as part of your exam time.

The introduction will include a sample screen display telling you to press 1, 2, 3 or 4 to select your answer or to press ? to mark for a later review. You then could press "enter" to record your answer before moving on to the next question. You may change your answer as often as you like before pressing enter. It is important to note that during the examination, the time remaining for your examination will be displayed at the top of the screen and updated as you record your answers. After you have answered every question in the examination, if you have time remaining, you will be given the opportunity to review all of the questions in the examination. You also will have the choice of reviewing only those questions that you marked for review or ending your examination and seeing your results. You may change your answers during the review options. You may repeat the review options as time allows.

It is important to emphasize that candidates taking the Real Estate Salesperson combined examination will be presented with the national and state questions in a single test session in which the questions appear in random order.

What To Expect on the Exam

Salesperson license applicants and broker license applicants will be given different exams. The salesperson's exam will be less difficult than the broker's. Questions will be in the form of four-answer multiple-choice problems such as this one:

The state of Wisconsin requires real estate license applicants to pass a test prior to licensure. This is to

1. keep people out of the real estate business.
2. raise revenue from test royalties.
3. raise revenue for real estate schools.
4. protect the public from unqualified persons attempting to practice sales and brokerage.

Generally, the test will include two types of questions—one tests your knowledge of general real estate and the other tests your ability to apply this knowledge to real estate problems.

Questions for the salesperson's exam are drawn from the following eight major areas.

Property ownership—a knowledge of characteristics affecting the acquisition and transfer of real estate. Included is an understanding of classes of property, land characteristics, encumbrances and types of ownership. Questions about property ownership make up approximately 12 percent of the salesperson's exam.

Law of agency—an understanding of what *agency* is, how it is created and terminated and the distinction between various kinds of agency relationships. Included is a knowledge of duties, responsibilities and legal obligations of an agent toward a principal and toward other parties. Questions on laws of agency compose approximately 20 percent of the exam.

Contracts—the knowledge of common contract terms, contract legal requirements and remedies in case of contract default, and basic features of contracts and options. Questions on contracts make up approximately 16 percent of the exam.

Federal laws and regulations—a knowledge of federal legislation dealing with fair housing, including the Civil Rights Act of 1964, the Fair Housing Act of 1968 and the Fair Housing Act Amendments of 1988. Questions on fair housing are approximately 15 percent of the exam.

Real estate mathematics—the ability to add, subtract, multiply and divide whole numbers, decimals and fractions. Also included is the ability to calculate land and building areas, real estate commissions and mortgage payments and an understanding of and ability to work with percentages. Questions on real estate mathematics compose approximately 10 percent of the exam.

Valuation and real estate economics—a knowledge of the methods used to estimate value. Included is an understanding of how economic and financial conditions affect real estate values. Questions on valuation and real estate economics constitute approximately 10 percent of the exam.

Financing—a knowledge of the financial aspects of real property transfer, including financial alternatives such as conventional and FHA mortgages, and the practices of financial institutions. Questions on financing make up approximately 10 percent of the exam.

Land-use controls and regulations—a knowledge of the kinds of restrictions that can be put on property use, including public restrictions—such as zoning ordinances and building codes—and private restrictions—such as deed restrictions. Questions on land-use controls and regulations constitute approximately 7 percent of the exam.

The state portion of the salesperson's exam includes content that has been approved by the Wisconsin Department of Regulation and Licensing. This portion pertains specifically to Wisconsin laws, principles and practices; it tests areas of knowledge that are required specifically for real estate salespeople licensed in Wisconsin. The state portion consists of 40 questions, including 14 questions on administrative rules, 12 questions on real-estate-related statutes and 14 questions on contractual forms.

Broker's examination. The Wisconsin real estate broker's exam consists of 100 multiple-choice questions. The exam tests the knowledge and skills required for real estate brokers licensed in Wisconsin. The content outline for the broker exam has been approved by the Wisconsin Department of Regulation and Licensing. Questions for the broker's exam are drawn from the following areas.

> Contracts—6 questions
> Approved forms—12 questions
> Trust accounts, escrow and closing statements—14 questions
> Business management and marketing—14 questions
> Financial and office management—12 questions
> Personnel—10 questions
> Business ethics—14 questions
> Consumer protection—16 questions
> Specialty areas—2 questions

The broker's exam lasts approximately 3.5 hours and includes several questions based on a settlement statement worksheet (closing statement).

In Chapter 23 of the *Wisconsin Supplement,* you worked through a closing problem based on a case history (or story) of a typical residential real estate transaction. The case history, the settlement statement worksheet and instructions on how to complete it and the accompanying questions at the end of the chapter are similar to what you will find on the examination. In computing prorations for these problems, you will be asked to base your computations on a particular method specified in the problem, which may not be the method you are accustomed to using. For example, a question may instruct you to compute a proration problem based on the actual number of days in the month of closing, with all calculations carried out to two decimal places. Follow the directions given in the problem exactly.

Salesperson's examination. The Wisconsin real estate salesperson's exam consists of 140 multiple-choice questions. The exam lasts approximately five hours. Like the broker's exam, it includes some questions based on closing statement prorations and computations. Also, salesperson applicants are expected to complete basic problems in real estate mathematics related to such topics as commissions, interest and area and volume.

Note that only non-programmable calculators that are silent, operate on batteries, have no paper tape printing capabilities and have no keyboard containing the alphabet will be permitted.

Sample questions. The questions on the exam are not set up to trick you. You will, however, encounter several exam questions that are more complex than the majority. Such questions are usually in a situational (story) format. You must read each question carefully to know exactly what is being asked before you begin to formulate your answer. Examples of some of the questions that seem to be the most difficult for examinees are illustrated in this section. These include questions with superfluous facts; questions asking for synthesis of facts; questions asking for reading comprehension, multistep math and value judgments; and best-answer questions.

Exam questions frequently contain superfluous facts that are not needed to answer the questions. For example:

The Koepkes paid $50,000 for their home five years ago and made a $10,000 down payment. Their monthly payments, including interest at 7¾ percent, amounted to $286. The interest portion of their last payment was $225.17. What was their approximate loan balance before their last payment?

The only facts you need to answer this question are the amount of the last interest payment and the rate of interest. To solve, you simply multiply the amount of the monthly interest, $225.17, by 12. You then divide the result by the interest rate, .0775, to get the approximate loan balance ($34,865.03).

Another type of question you will find on the test asks you to take facts that you have learned separately and synthesize that information to answer the question. For example:

Twelve years ago, the Paul Zieglers, parents of two children, retired and left Madison, Wisconsin, taking up residence in Alabama along the Gulf Coast. They decided to keep their Madison residence, which they owned as tenants in common, renting to friends. Mae Ziegler died suddenly, leaving no will. Alabama law provides that when a wife dies intestate, a widower receives a life estate in all real property owned by his wife at death. Paul will inherit which of the following interests in the Madison home?

1.   In severalty due to the right of survivorship
2.   A life estate
3.   One-half of the interest
4.   The entire estate

The correct answer is 4. To answer this question, you need to know: (1) that rights of survivorship do not apply to a tenancy in common; (2) that Wisconsin property is probated in Wisconsin in accordance with Wisconsin law; (3) that the laws of descent apply because the wife died intestate; (4) what the laws of descent are in Wisconsin; and (5) how to combine numerically the real estate interest held before and after the wife's death.

The third type of question you may find on the test requires you to read each word extremely carefully for comprehension. For example:

Closing of a transaction for a residential property is set for April 19, 1989. Seller has a three-year insurance policy that expires June 25, 1990. Seller has prepaid a three-year premium of $555. Buyer is to take over the policy as of the date of closing. The closing credited to the buyer at closing is

1. $185.00.
2. $202.99.
3. $231.25.
4.   None of the above

The answer here is 4 because the prorated amount of the prepaid insurance would be debited to the buyer.

Another type of question that frequently appears on PSI exams is the multistep math question. For example:

Karen Valentine bought a house at exactly the appraised value. She negotiated a loan through Prairieville Savings and Loan Association at 75 percent of the appraised value. The interest rate was 9 percent. The first month's interest was $405. What was the selling price of the property?

To answer this question, you must first multiply $405 by 12 to get the annual interest ($4,860). You then divide $4,860 by the interest rate, .09, to get the amount of the loan ($54,000). Next, you divide $54,000 by .75 to find the appraised value ($72,000), which is the same as the purchase price.

A few questions on the exam may ask you to make a value judgment. For example:

Broker Howard Smedloe listed a small house owned by George Miller at $26,000, obtaining an executed sales contract on it within six weeks at $25,000. Smedloe learned there was an existing $15,000 first mortgage and a $5,000 second mortgage on the property. Smedloe knew the real estate could be refinanced on a new $20,000 first-mortgage loan. The holder of the second mortgage, Peter Frye, told Smedloe he was willing to discount his $5,000 note, selling it for $4,500. The buyer has $5,000 cash and qualifies for a new $20,000 first-mortgage loan. Smedloe should

1.   say nothing to Miller about refinancing and allow the transaction to close.
2.   tell Miller the second mortgage can be paid off at a $500 discount.
3.   tell Frye the property is sold and therefore he should demand the full amount of $5,000.
4.   buy the second mortgage himself at the $500 discount.

The answer of course is 2. As an agent of the seller, the broker must act in the seller's best interest. Furthermore, alternative 4 would be illegal because the broker would become a principal in the transaction without informing anyone.

You frequently will be asked to choose the best answer from alternatives when the ideal answer is not present. For example:

Broker Marmon Lowrie listed Louise Navarro's beachfront home at $142,500. Three weeks later, Lowrie was fortunate to obtain a full-price offer on the beach house from Scott Lasser. Stopping by the house after the sales contract was executed and in force, Lowrie was appalled to see a large foundation crack. Two days later, Lowrie noticed the crack had been repaired carefully. Lowrie knew that seller Navarro was unaware of the crack because she had extremely poor eyesight. Lowrie suspected that the crack had been fixed by Navarro's son-in-law, a building contractor. Lowrie should

1.   disclose the fact of the crack to buyer Lasser.
2.   immediately cancel the sales contract.
3.   keep quiet about the crack because it had been repaired.
4.   confront the son-in-law with his suspicions and threaten to sue.

The best alternative available here is *1*. The better answer, "inform seller Navarro of the crack, requesting permission to inform buyer Lasser," does not appear here. Note that this question also asks you to make a value judgment.

Preparing for the License Examination

We have tried to prepare you for the Wisconsin real estate licensing examination by including in the *Wisconsin Supplement* the kinds of items usually found on the test. Your most important preparation for the test involves studying real estate principles, practices and laws. Concentrate on learning the material by studying both *Modern Real Estate Practice* and the *Wisconsin Supplement* and by working all the tests and exercises, paying particularly close attention to those problems you may have missed originally. Of course, you also should study the book published by the Department of Regulation and Licensing. Remember, you will be asked to apply your knowledge to situations, combining facts and principles as illustrated in this chapter.

TAKING THE LICENSE EXAMINATION

For best results, you should go through the entire examination first and answer those questions you are certain about, leaving the doubtful ones for last. This way, you at least will avoid missing a question you know through lack of time. After you have answered all the questions you know for certain, return to the remaining questions. If you are unable to arrive at an answer the second time through, guess. There is no penalty for guessing.

One of the most important assets in taking an examination is to remain relaxed. If you are nervous, your mind may not function as well as it should and you might have difficulty with the material. If you are prepared and have an adequate knowledge of the subject, you should be able to complete the examination successfully.

Answer Key

The following answers are referenced to pages in each chapter where points are discussed or explained. These references are made to help you make maximum use of the tests. If you did not answer a question correctly, restudy the course material until you understand the correct answer.

Chapter 4
1. 2(1)
2. 4(2)
3. 3(2)
4. 4(3)
5. 3(3)
6. 2(3)
7. 4(4)
8. 2(4)
9. 2(4)
10. 3(3)

Chapter 5
1. 4(8)
2. 1(8)
3. 4(9)
4. 2(9)
5. 4(9)
6. 4(9)
7. 2(9)
8. 2(9)
9. 1(9)
10. 1(9)
11. 4(8)

Chapter 6
1. 3(17)
2. 1(17)
3. 3(18)
4. 3(18)
5. 3(18)
6. 3(17)

Chapter 7
1. 2(20)
2. 2(20)
3. 2(22)
4. 2(20)
5. 2(21)
6. 3(21)
7. 3(22)
8. 1(22)

Chapter 8
1. 4(24)
2. 2(24)
3. 2(25)
4. 3(26)
5. 3(26)
6. 4(24)

Chapter 9
1. 4(29)
2. 4(29)
3. 4(29)
4. 3(28)
5. 3(28)
6. 2(31)
7. 3(30)
8. 2(28)
9. 4(28)
10. 3(29)
11. 4(30)

Chapter 10
1. 4(33)
2. 3(33)
3. 1(34)
4. 1(35)
5. 1(35)
6. 2(36)
7. 4(39)
8. 3(38)
9. 3(38)
10. 2(36)
11. 3(36)

Chapter 11
1. 3(46)
2. 3(47)
3. 4(46)
4. 4(47)

**Chapter 11
(continued)**
5. 4(48)
6. 3(49)
7. 2(50)
8. 4(50)
9. 2(48)
10. 4(49)
11. 2(49)

Chapter 12
1. 3(52)
2. 1(52)
3. 4(52)
4. 2(52)
5. 1(52)
6. 1(54)

Chapter 13
1. 2(57)
2. 3(56)
3. 4(59)
4. 4(59)
5. 2(60)
6. 3(61)
7. 4(61)
8. 4(63)
9. 3(62)
10. 2(57)
11. 2(62)
12. 4(59)
13. 2(61)
14. 4(60)
15. 1(63)
16. 4(61)
17. 1(62)
18. 3(63)
19. 4(57)
20. 3(61)
21. 4(63)

Chapter 14/15
1. 1(69)
2. 3(69)
3. 4(70)
4. 3(73)
5. 3(69,75)
6. 4(69)
7. 2(75)
8. 3(75)

Chapter 16
1. 3(78)
2. 1(79)
3. 2(79)
4. 3(81)
5. 1(81)
6. 3(81)
7. 2(78)

Chapter 19/20
1. 3(83)
2. 4(83)
3. 1(83)
4. 2(83)
5. 2(84)
6. 4(85)

Chapter 23
1. 4(88)
2. 2(104)
3. 4(88)
4. 2(88)
5. 2(104)
6. 4(104)
7. 2(105)
8. 1(105)
9. 3(105)
10. 1(91)

Form 930-B
Rev. 4/85

Buyer's Closing Statement

Nelco Forms
P.O. Box 10208
Green Bay, WI 54307-0208
414-337-1000

Broker

NEW HOUSE REALTY

Property Location　　1400 Regas Lane, Madison, WI 53703

Seller(s)
(Name and address)　　George and Martha Carter

Buyer(s)
(Name and address)　　Jay and Linda Jones

Contract date　11-15-94　　Closing date　12-15-94　　Closed at

BUYER'S SETTLEMENT WITH BROKER	Due Seller		Credit Buyer	
1. Sale price	$ 56,000	00		
2. Earnest money paid by Buyer			$ 4,000	00
3. Downpayment by Buyer (in addition to Earnest money)............................				
4. Mortgages or land contracts assumed by Buyer:				
Principal $26,354.27　　Interest $80.87			26,435	14
5. Trust funds due Seller held by mortgagee:				
*6. Delinquent taxes assumed for years				
*7. Seller's share of taxes for 1994 prorated from 1-1-94 to 12-15-94, prorated on a 365 basis @ $ 3.35 per day, to be paid by Buyer (Last Year's taxes were $ 1,224.00)....................			1,166	47
*8. Future installments of special assessment assumed by Buyer				
9. Rent prorated (see below)				
10. Fuel oil and other items on premises:	80	00		
*11. Recording fees				
*12. Real estate transfer fees				
13. Insurance Premium Prorated	178	10		
14.				
15.				
16. 　　　　**TOTALS**...	$ 56,258	10	$ 31,601	61
17. Credits to Buyer (Enter total of second column on line 16)	31,601	61		
18. Balance due from Buyer (Line 16 less line 17)................................	$ 24,656	49		
19. Less: Mortgage or land contract executed by Buyer to Seller				
Other:				
20. Check or cash from Buyer to Broker (Line 18 less line 19)	$ 24,656	49		

TENANT'S NAME	MONTHLY RENTAL	PAYABLE	DATE PAID UP TO	PRORATED AMOUNT

*This item could appear on the closing statement between the Broker and Seller but not on both.

Use and Occupancy - Broker will escrow $ _____ for use and occupancy charge and $ _____ to guarantee delivery of possession to Buyer until the property is vacated by the Seller, which includes the day of vacating. Any balance of the escrow money will be returned to the Seller upon vacating and delivery of keys to Broker.

Daily use and occupancy charge is $ _____. Date of vacating this property will be _____

Other - Seller certifies that he will leave all non-real estate items on the premises as agreed upon in the purchase agreement. Seller shall have all meters read prior to vacating and agrees to pay any delinquent or outstanding bills promptly upon receipt of such bill.

THIS STATEMENT IS ACCEPTED AS CORRECT _____ , 19 ____

_____ Buyer　　　　_____ Seller

_____ Buyer　　　　_____ Seller

930B NTF 0056B

Form 930-S
Rev. 4 86

Seller's Closing Statement

Nelco Forms
P.O. Box 10208
Green Bay, WI 54307-0208
414-337-1000

Broker

NEW HOUSE REALTY

Property Location _____ 1400 Regas Lane, Madison, WI 53705 _____

Seller(s)
(Name and address) __ George and Martha Carter __

Buyer(s)
(Name and address) __ Jay and Linda Jones __
Contract date __ 11-15-94 __ Closing date __ 12-15-94 __ Closed at _____

BROKER'S SETTLEMENT WITH SELLER	Charges against Seller		Due Seller	
1. Check or cash received from Buyer (line 20 of Form 930-B)			$ 26,656	49
2. Earnest money and down payment received from Buyer			4,000	00
3. Total Amount Due Seller before charges against Seller (Line 1 plus line 2)			$ 28,656	49
4. Abstract extention or title policy _____	$ 318	50		
*5. Recording fees __ Deed __				
	10	00		
*6. Real estate transfer fee . $56,000 x .003	168	10		
7. Attorney fees paid to __ Deed Preparation __				
	90	00		
8. Mortgage or land contract paid by Broker _____				
*9. Delinquent taxes paid by Broker for years _____				
*10. Seller's share of taxes for ____ prorated from ____ to ____ , prorated on a ____ basis @ $ ____ per ____ , to be paid by Broker (Last Year's taxes were $ ____)				
*11. Special assessments paid by Broker _____				
12. Other advances by Broker _____				
13. Commission .$56,000 x .07.	3,920	00		
14. Services by Broker (Itemize) _____				
15. Water Meter Reading 12-15-94	20	00		
16. _____				
17. _____				
18. _____				
19. _____				
20. _____				
21. **TOTAL Charges Against Seller**	$ 4,526	50		
22. Balance Due Seller (Line 3 less line 21)			$ 24,129	99

*This item could appear on the closing statment between the Buyer and Broker but not on both.

Use and Occupancy - Broker will escrow $ _____ for use and occupancy charge and $ _____ to guarantee delivery of possession to Buyer until the property is vacated by the Seller, which includes the day of vacating. Any balance of the escrow money will be returned to the Seller upon vacating and delivery of keys to Broker.

Daily use and occupancy charge is $ _____ . Date of vacating this property will be _____

Other - Seller certifies that he will leave all non-real estate items on the premises as agreed upon in the purchase agreement. Seller shall have all meters read prior to vacating and agrees to pay any delinquent or outstanding bills promptly upon receipt of such bill.

THIS STATEMENT IS ACCEPTED AS CORRECT _____ , 19 _____

_____ Broker _____ Seller

By _____ _____ Seller

930S NTF 0057C

Index

A

Acceleration clauses, 75, 76
Acceptance, 34, 41
Acknowledgment, 47
Addenda, 15
Address, change of, 61
Adverse possession, 47
Advertising, 11, 64–65
Agency
  creation of, 1
  disclosure form, 3–4
  law, 3–6
American Land Title Association
  (ALTA), 53
Apprentice salesperson
  activities, 62
  definition of, 57
Assessment
  for property taxes, 28
  special, 29
Assessor certification program,
  30–31
Assignee, 70
Assignment
  of land contract, 76
  of mortgage, 70
Automatic extension clauses, 80

B

Balloon payments, 75
Blind ads, 11
Branch office, 61
Broker
  agency law, 3–6
  authority to prepare documents, 33
  client funds, handling of, 62–63
  commission, 1–2, 13, 14
    determination of, 2
    payment of, 12
  definition of, 56–57
  liability of, 6
  licensing
    examination, 59–60, 97–102
    requirements, 59
  multiple representation by, 1
  relationship
    with independent contractor, 2–3
    with salesperson, 2–3
    with seller, 1
  responsibilities of
    licensure duties, 59
    for own statements, 3

role
  at closing, 88
  and earnest money, 40
  as marketing agent, 12, 13
  roster, 58
Brokerage, 1–6
Building code, 86
Bulk sales affidavit, 54
Bulk transfers, 54
Business
  offers form, 53
  operation of, 61–65
  place of, 61
  sale transaction, 53, 54
Buyer
  closing statement, 91–93, 94
  inspections, 40, 42
  owner's title insurance policy, 88
  role at closing, 88

C

Cemetery
  brokers, 57
  salespeople, 57
Certification, assessor, 30–31
Chattel, 53
Closing, 88–91
  escrow, 44
Closing statement
  buyer's, 91–93
    sample, 94
  completion of, 89–91
  seller's, 93, 96
    sample, 95
Code of Ethics, 2
Commercial lease, 80
Commingling, 63
Commission, 64
  broker, 1–2, 12, 13, 14
  calculations, 90
  independent contractor, 2
Common-law property system, 20, 35
Community property system, 20
Competent parties, 34
Compliance, certificate of, 50
Condition report, 5–6, 14, 15
Condominium
  associations, 22–23
  conversion, 22
  ownership, 22–23
Condominium Ownership Act, 22
Confidentiality, 3

Confidentiality statement, 4
Consent, irrevocable, 61
Conservation easements, 18
Consideration, 34
Construction lien, 29–30
Constructive notice, 52, 54
Contingencies, 40
Contract
  delivery of, 62
  forms, 33
  independent contractor's, 2–3
  installment, 44
  land, 44, 75–76
  listing, 1, 8
    changes to form, 12
    explanation of, 11, 13–16
    sample, 9–10
  offer to purchase
    changes to form, 40
    explanation of, 41–44
    sample, 36–39
  statute of limitations, 44
  sweetheart, 22
  terms of, 34–35
  validity of, 34
Co-ownership, 20
Corporation, licensing, 60
Counteroffer, 34
County park commission, 83
Curtesy, 17–18

D

Deed, 47
  form of, 34
  recording of, 52
  trust, 69
Default, 42
Deferred marital property, 21
Deficiency judgment, 76
Delivery, 41, 62
Demand, 11
Disclosure
  of adverse facts, 5
  agency form, 3–4
  condominium sales, 22
  full, 3
  by seller, 5–6
Discrimination, disclosure and, 5
Documents
  foreign language, 52
  preparation of, 33, 64
  recording, 52

Dower, 17–18
Dual agency, 1, 14

E
Earnest money
  broker's role in, 40
  disbursement of, 42
  disputes involving, 43
  handling of, 43
  holding of, 42
  provisions for, 12, 16
Easement, 18
  negative utility, 12
  by prescription, 18
Education
  continuing, 59
  licensure requirements, 59
Encumbrances, 35
Environmental controls, 86
Environmental impact statements, 86
Equitable conversion, doctrine of, 34
Equity interest, 75
Escrow, 70
  agent, 44
  closing, 44
Estate
  in land, 17
  for years, 78, 79
Ethical practices, 3, 4–5
Ethics, Code of, 2, 64
Eviction, 80
Exclusive buyer agency contract, 1
Exclusive-right-to-sell listing, 8
  sample contract, 9–10
Exculpatory clause, 79–80

F
Farmland Preservation Act, 85
Farmland-preservation agreement, 85
Farm lease, 80
Fee simple, 34
Fee-splitting, 64
Financing, 43
  consumer protection legislation, 74–75
  land contracts, 75–76
  mortgages, 69–75
Fixtures
  list of, 12, 13, 40, 43
  trade, 53
Floodplain, 85
Foreclosure
  land contract, 76
  mortgage, 69
Foreign language documents, 52
Forms
  6-L (mortgage document), 69, 71–72
  WB-1 (residential listing contract), 11–16
  WB-11 (residential offer to purchase), 36–44
  WB-36 (exclusive buyer agency contract), 1
  WB-43 (amendment to contract of sale), 34

WB-44 (counteroffer form), 34
WB-46 (counteroffer form), 34
"For sale" signs, 65
Fourth Principal Meridian, 24
Funds
  handling of, 62–63
  record keeping, 63–64

G/H
Gross lease, 80
Hearing
  in lieu of, 66
  right to, 66
Holdover tenancy, 78
Homeowners' Warranty (HOW)
    Program, 86
Homestead, 17, 35
Housing and Neighborhood
    Conservation Program (HNCP), 74
Hunting rights, 18

I/J
Independent contractor, 2–3
Individual property, 20–21
Inspections, 4–5, 42
Installment contracts, 44
Insurance
  mortgage provisions, 70
  prorations, 90
  title, 53, 88
Intestate, 46
Joint tenancy, 21, 22
Judgments, 30
Judicial foreclosure, 69, 76

L
Land contract, 44
  assignment of, 76
  consumer protection legislation, 75
  forfeiture of, 76
  forms, 75
  recording of, 75
Landlord
  breach of lease by, 79–80
  remedies available to, 79
*Landlords and Tenants—The
    Wisconsin Way,* 81
Land trust, 23
Land use, 83–86
Lease, 34
  automatic extension clauses, 80
  breach of
    by landlord, 79–80
    by tenant, 79
  forms, 78
  recording of, 78–79
  statute of frauds, 78
  termination of, 79
  types of, 80
  validity of, 78–79
Leasehold estates, 78
Legal description, 24–26
  and contracts, 34
  and listing contract, 12, 13
  and offer to purchase, 40

Legal life estate, 17
Legislation
  financing, 74–75
  land contracts, 75
License
  applications, 58–59
  broker-employer duties, 59
  continuing-education requirements, 59
  corporations, 60
  education requirements, 59
  examination, 59–60, 97–102
  fees, 60
  issuing of, 60
  law, 1, 56
    business operation provisions, 61–65
    definitions under, 56–58
    exceptions to, 57–58
    licensing procedures, 58–61
    nonresident, 60–61
    partnerships, 60
    reissue of, 66
    renewal, 61
    requirements, 58–59
    suspension/revocation of, 65–66
    transfer of, 62
Licensee
  address change, 61
  advertising regulations, 64–65
  conduct of, 4–5
  duties of, 3–4
  ethical practices, 4–5
  legal advice to, 64
  multiple representation, 4
  obligations to public, 64
Lien, 29–30
Lien-theory, 69
Lis pendens, 54
Listing
  agreements, 8–16
  considerations, 11
  contract, 1, 8, 9–10
    changes in, 12
    explanation of, 11–16
    extension of, 12, 14–15
    termination of, 11
    types of, 8
Litigation, 14
Loss, risk of, 44

M
Marital agreement, 46
Marital property, 18, 20–22, 35, 40
Marital Property Act, 35, 40
  property classifications under, 40
  spouse acting alone under, 35, 40
Master plan, 83
Material supplier, 30
Mechanics' lien, 29–30
Metes and bounds description, 24
Mill, 28
Minor, and contracts, 34
Misrepresentation, 3, 4
Mixed property, 21

Mobile homes, 6
Mortgage, 69
  assignment of, 70
  bankers, 57
  document, sample, 71–72
  foreclosure, 69
  forms, 69
  insurance provisions, 70
  loan instruments, 69
  prepayment of, 70
  property tax provisions, 70
  satisfaction of, 69
  title insurance policy, 88
  usury law, 70
  veteran's programs, 73–74
Multiple representation, 1, 4

N
National Association of REALTORS®,
    2
Net lease, 80
Nonassignment clauses, 76
Nonjudicial foreclosure, 69
Nonresident, licensing, 60–61
Note, 69
Notice, 79
  constructive, 52, 54
  delivery of, 79
  of lien, 29–30
  to vacate, 79

O
Occupancy, 41
Occupancy date, 13
Offer, 34, 41
Offer to purchase, 33
  changes to form, 40
  contingencies/conditions, 35
  explanation of, 41–44
  sample, 36–39
  terms of, 34–35
Out-of-state unimproved properties,
    84
Override clause, 8, 12
Ownership, 20–23

P
Partition, suit for, 20
Partnership, 23, 60
Payment, method of, 34
Percentage lease, 80
Periodic tenancy, 78, 79
Personal property
  and business sale transaction, 53
  mobile homes as, 6
  included in sale, 35
Plan commissions, 83
Plat, of subdivision, 24, 26, 83–84
Potential, 11
Prepayment
  penalty, 70, 73
  privileges, 75
Prime contractor, 29
Prior appropriation, doctrine of,
    18–19

Property
  classifications of, 21, 40
  condition report, 42
  destruction of, 80
  holding, 35
  individual, 20–21
  marital, 18, 20–22, 35, 40
  personal, 6, 35, 53
  real, 6
Property tax, 30–31
  assessment, 28
  delinquency, 29
  exemptions, 28
  levy, 28
  mortgage provisions for, 70
  payment, 29
  prorations, 91
  rate, 28
Prorations, 40–42, 90–91
Public easements, 18
Public trust doctrine, 18
Puffing, 3

R
Real estate
  business, 61–65
  interests in, 17–19
  tax, 28–29, 30–31, 70, 91
  transfer fee, 47–48
Real property, 6
Record keeping, 63–64
Recording
  of deed, 47
  documents, 52
  of lease, 78–79
Rectangular survey, 24
Redemption, 29
  equitable right of, 70
  period, 70, 76
Rental Unit Energy Efficiency Code,
    50
Rental weatherization requirements,
    48–50
Residential Rental Practices Code,
    80–81
Restraining orders, 66
Restrictions, 35
Revocation, of license, 65–66
Riparian right doctrine, 18
Rural homestead, 17

S
Salesperson
  definition of, 57
  licensing
    examination, 59–60, 97–102
    requirements, 59
  relationship with broker, 2–3
  roster, 58
  termination of employment, 61–62
Scenic easements, 18
Security agreements, 54
Security deposit, 81
Seller
  closing statement, 93, 95–96

cooperation of, 13–14
disclosure law, 5–6
duties of, 13
reason for selling, 11
relationship with broker, 1
responsibilities of, 15
role at closing, 88
Shoreland zoning, 84–85
Signatures, 35, 40
Small Claims Court, 43
Special assessments, 29, 42
Special-use permits, 83
Spouse, surviving, 46
Statute of limitations, 44
Statutory redemption period, 70
Stipulation, 50
Strict foreclosure, 69, 76
Subcontractor, 30
Subdivision
  lot and block description, 24
  out-of-state lot marketing, 84
  plats, 83–84
  regulations, 83–84
Succession, 46
Supply, 11
Survey, 83, 88
Survivorship marital property, 21, 22
Suspension, of license, 65–66
Sweetheart contracts, 22

T
Tax
  assessors, 30–31
  proration, 42
  real estate. *See* Property tax
  sale, 29
Tenancy
  in common, 21, 22
  at sufferance, 78
  at will, 78, 79
Tenant
  breach of lease by, 79
  periodic, 79
  remedies available to, 79
Time is of the essence, 34, 41
Time-share, salesperson, 57
Title
  abstract, 52, 88
  claim of, 47
  cloud on, 54
  equitable, 34
  evidence of, 13, 43, 52, 88
  form of, 42
  insurance, 53, 88
  records, 52–54
  transfer of, 46–50
  warranty of, 42
Torrens system, 53
Township map, 25
Transfer
  authorization, 50
  bulk, 54
  fee, 47–48
  of title, 46–50
Trust accounts, 62–63

disbursements from, 63–64
record keeping, 63–64
rule revisions for, 63
Trust deed, 69

U
Uniform Building Code, 86
Uniform Commercial Code, 33, 54
Uniform Limited Partnership Act, 23
Uniform Marital Property Act, 20
Uniform Partnership Act, 23
Uniform Vendor and Purchaser Risk
    Act, 44
Unit ownerships, 22
Urban homestead, 17
Usury, 70

V/W
Value, assessed, 28
Variances, 83
Veterans loan programs
    first-mortgage, 73
    home improvement, 74
Voluntary alienation, 47–50
Waiver, 40
Water rights, 18–19
Weatherization standards, 48–50
Wills, 46
Wisconsin Consumer Act, 74–75
    exemptions, 75
    land contracts and, 75
Wisconsin Department of
    Agriculture, Trade and Consumer
    Protection
    on advertising, 64–65

Residential Rental Practices
    Code, 80–81
Wisconsin Department of
    Development, 83–84
Wisconsin Department of Health, 84
Wisconsin Department of Industry,
    Labor and Human Relations
Wisconsin Department of Natural
    Resources (DNR), 19
    and floodplain regulations, 85
    and shoreland regulations, 84–85
Wisconsin Department of Regulation
    and Licensing, 1, 2
    application form, 58–59
    business offers form, 53
    contract forms, 33
    examinations, 58
    lease forms, 78
    license transfer, 62
    mortgage forms, 69
Wisconsin Department of Revenue
    assessor certification, 30–31
Wisconsin Department of
    Transportation
    subdivision plats and, 84
Wisconsin Department of Veterans
    Affairs
    home improvement loan program, 74
    home-loan programs, 73
Wisconsin Environmental Policy Act
    (WEPA), 86
Wisconsin Housing and Economic
    Development Authority
    (WHEDA) loan programs, 74

Wisconsin Law of Intestate
    Succession, 46
Wisconsin Marital Property Act, 18,
    20–22
Wisconsin Property Assessment
    Manual, 31
Wisconsin Real Estate Board, 2
    on advertising, 11
    duties/powers of, 58
    functions of, 56
    members of, 58
    organization of, 58
    rosters, 58
Wisconsin REALTORS® Association, 2
Wisconsin State Bar Association
    contract forms, 33
    mortgage assignment forms, 70
    mortgage document forms, 70
    mortgage forms, 69
Wisconsin Statute of Frauds, 34, 78
Wisconsin Subdivision Code, 83
Wisconsin Unfair Trade Practices
    Act, 81

Z
Zoning, 83
    amendments, 83
    board of adjustment, 83
    committee, 83
    exclusive agricultural use, 85
    floodplain, 85
    ordinances, 83
    shoreland, 84–85

Get the Performance Advantage on the job...*in the classroom*

Order Number		Real Estate Principles and Exam Preparation	Qty.	Price	Total Amount
1.	1510-01	Modern Real Estate Practice, 13th edition	_____	$36.95	_____
2.	1516-01	Key Point Review Audio Tapes for Modern Real Estate Practice, 13th ed.	_____	$28.95	_____
3.	1510-02	Study Guide for Modern Real Estate Practice, 13th edition	_____	$13.95	_____
4.	1961-01	Language of Real Estate, 4th edition	_____	$28.95	_____
5.	1610-07	Real Estate Math, 4th edition	_____	$15.95	_____
6.	1512-10	Mastering Real Estate Mathematics, 5th edition	_____	$25.95	_____
7.	1970-04	Questions & Answers To Help You Pass the Real Estate Exam, 4th edition	_____	$21.95	_____
8.	1516-02	Real Estate Exam Preparation Software—5 1/4" IBM-Compatible Disk	_____	$35.00	_____
9.	1516-03	Real Estate Exam Preparation Software—3 1/2" IBM-Compatible Disk	_____	$35.00	_____
10.	1970-06	Real Estate Exam Guide: ASI, 3rd edition	_____	$21.95	_____
11.	1970-09	Guide to Passing the PSI Real Estate Exam	_____	$21.95	_____
12.	1970-08	New York Real Estate Exam Guide	_____	$21.95	_____
13.	1970-03	How to Prepare for the Texas Real Estate Exam, 5th ed.	_____	$19.50	_____

Advanced Study/Specialty Areas

			Qty.	Price	Total Amount
14.	1520-02	ADA Handbook: Employment and Construction Issues Affecting Your Business	_____	$29.95	_____
15.	1560-08	Agency Relationships in Real Estate, 2nd edition	_____	$25.95	_____
16.	1978-03	Buyer Agency: Your Competitive Edge Real Estate, 2nd edition	_____	$24.95	_____
17.	1557-10	Essentials of Real Estate Finance, 7th edition	_____	$38.95	_____
18.	1559-01	Essentials of Real Estate Investment, 4th edition	_____	$38.95	_____
19.	1556-10	Fundamentals of Real Estate Appraisal, 6th edition	_____	$38.95	_____
20.	1556-14	How to Use the Uniform Residential Appraisal Report, 2nd edition	_____	$24.95	_____
21.	1556-15	Introduction to Income Property Appraisal	_____	$34.95	_____
22.	1556-11	Language of Real Estate Appraisal	_____	$21.95	_____
23.	1557-15	Modern Residential Financing Methods, 2nd edition	_____	$19.95	_____
24.	1551-10	Property Management, 4th edition	_____	$35.95	_____
25.	1556-12	Questions & Answers to Help You Pass the Real Estate Appraisal Exams	_____	$26.95	_____
26.	1560-01	Real Estate Law, 3rd edition	_____	$38.95	_____
27.	1556-18	Uniform Standards of Professional Appraisal Practice, 2nd edition	_____	$19.95	_____

Sales & Marketing/Professional Development

			Qty.	Price	Total Amount
28.	1913-04	Close for Success	_____	$18.95	_____
29.	1913-15	Houses	_____	$19.95	_____
30.	1907-06	How to Develop a Six-Figure Income in Real Estate	_____	$22.95	_____
31.	4105-09	How to Profit in Commercial Real Estate Investing	_____	$34.95	_____
32.	1913-01	List for Success	_____	$18.95	_____
33.	5608-89	Multiply Your Success with Real Estate Assistants	_____	$79.95	_____
34.	1909-06	New Home Selling Strategies: A Handbook for Success	_____	$24.95	_____
35.	1913-11	Phone Power	_____	$19.95	_____
36.	1907-05	Power Real Estate Advertising	_____	$24.95	_____
37.	1926-03	Power Real Estate Letters	_____	$29.95	_____
38.	1926-10	Power Real Estate Letters w/ 5 1/4" IBM-Compatible Disk	_____	$79.95	_____
39.	1926-09	Power Real Estate Letters w/ 3/1/2" IBM-Compatible Disk	_____	$79.95	_____
40.	1907-01	Power Real Estate Listing, 2nd edition	_____	$18.95	_____
41.	1907-04	Power Real Estate Negotiation	_____	$19.95	_____
42.	1907-02	Power Real Estate Selling, 2nd edition	_____	$18.95	_____
43.	1907-07	Real Estate Agent's Guide to Listing and Sales Success	_____	$22.95	_____
44.	1965-01	Real Estate Brokerage: A Success Guide, 3rd edition	_____	$35.95	_____
45.	5608-71	Real Estate Investor's Tax Guide	_____	$24.95	_____
46.	1913-13	The Real Estate Sales Survival Kit.	_____	$24.95	_____
47.	1978-02	Recruiting Revolution in Real Estate	_____	$34.95	_____
48.	1903-31	Sold! The Professional's Guide to Real Estate Auctions	_____	$32.95	_____

Book total _____
Tax _____
Shipping and Handling _____
Less $1.00 off if you fax order _____
Total amount _____

Real Estate Education Company

Where Experts Begin

a division of Dearborn Financial Publishing, Inc.

520 North Dearborn Street, Chicago, IL 60610-4354

Return Address:

_____

_____

_____

IMPORTANT—PLEASE FOLD OVER—PLEASE TAPE BEFORE MAILING

Your Satisfaction is Guaranteed!
All books come with a 30-day
money-back guarantee. If you are not
completely satisfied, simply return your
books in saleable condition and your
money will be refunded in full.

FOR YOUR CONVENIENCE!

NOTE: This page, when folded over and taped, becomes a mailing
envelope. When paying by check, please seal/tape on three sides.

**Real Estate
Education Company**
a division of Dearborn Financial Publishing, Inc.